Piano Chords One
(All Seven Natural Keys)

A Beginner's Guide To Simple Music Theory
and Playing Chords To Any Song Quickly

MICAH BROOKS

WORSHIPHEART
PUBLISHING | EST. 1985

Also By Micah Brooks

The Guitar Authority Series:

Worship Guitar In Six Weeks:
A Complete Beginner's Guide to Learning
Rhythm Guitar for Christian Worship Music

42 Guitar Chords Everyone Should Know:
A Complete Step-By-Step Guide To Mastering
42 Of The Most Important Guitar Chords

Guitar Secrets Revealed:
Unconventional and Amazing Guitar Chords,
Professional Techniques, Capo Tricks,
Alternate Tunings, Head Math, Rhythm & More

Songbooks and Music:

Micah Brooks All Things New EP Songbook

Micah Brooks All Things New EP

Devotional Books:

21 Day Character Challenge:
A Daily Devotional and Bible Reading Plan

Galatians: A Fresh, New Six Day
Bible Study and Commentary

Ephesians: A Fresh, New Six Day
Bible Study and Commentary

James: A Fresh, New Five Day
Bible Study and Commentary

Your Free Invitation

I hope to add value to your life through this piano book. I know that the first few chapters would be much easier to master if we could meet together in person. Because we all live throughout the world, this isn't always possible. Instead, with the purchase of *Piano Chords One* I'm offering a free (no strings attached) video phone call with me that will help you get going. I'll walk you through the vital first steps you'll need to be successful while learning the material in this book. We'll also be able to make a connection in case you have questions moving forward. I love meeting my readers and want you to enjoy this process. Visit: micahbrooks.com/invitation to set up your time to meet with me.

Thank you and blessings,
Micah Brooks

Micah Brooks

Copyright Information

Published by WorshipHeart Publishing

Dedication

It's my honor and privilege to dedicate this book to everyone at Providence Christian Academy in Murfreesboro, Tennessee [USA]. While I'm only an adjunct educator at your school, your welcoming love and support have blessed not only myself but also my family. Thank you and may this book and others like it bless our community as well as new piano players around the world.

Micah Brooks

Contents

Introduction

Jumpy Frog songs or what?

The best thing about teaching guitar lessons is how fast a student can learn to play a song. If you'll learn the G, C, D, and Em chords, you can play most pop songs. For centuries, the piano hasn't been taught with this kind of out-of-the-gate launch speed. Most piano teachers begin by teaching music notes, then scales, then right-hand technique, then left-hand, etc. It can take up to six weeks before you begin playing your first song. Plus, most teachers use *intro to piano* or method books. A friend of mine appropriately named the songs within them *jumpy frog* songs. These are the type that the red bouncing ball would have accompanied in elementary school TV shows in the 1980s. Jumpy frog songs are boring! It's time to bring the play-a-song-from-day-one guitar method to the piano. I've used this technique with many students and the success rate is just as high as with those who have learned guitar.

So, why don't most piano instructors teach using this piano chord method? There are two answers to this question. First, it's what they know. In other words, it's how they were taught when they first learned the instrument. They're comfortable with the process. The second reason is that it takes a skilled and *patient* teacher to know just how fast to move with each particular student. Each individual has to be properly evaluated. When using a jumpy frog method book, you move at the pace of the book itself. The lesson plan is already spelled out. In reality, the teacher only needs to know a little bit more than the student. In essence, an eight-year-old could teach a seven-year-old to play the piano using a well prepared jumpy frog book.

So, what about all of the traditional stuff? What about learning music notation, left and right-hand technique, and so on? You do need to know this material, but it can be discovered as you go. Instead of spending six weeks talking about the piano, we're going to spend six weeks playing songs.

Another question you may have is about playing Beethoven, Bach, and Schumann. The classical piano teacher has me beat on this one. This piano chord method isn't about sight-reading sheet music. That's what traditional piano lessons do best. Rather, this is for people who want play piano or keyboard on a worship team or in a pop, country, or rock band. This method is for singer-songwriters and creative musicians. It's for those who want to hear a song on the radio and have the tools to play it. If you want to create your own music, this is the way to start!

It's time to resist the urge to use jumpy frog piano books and launch out into the deep. It's time to be a creative musician. We will even be able to play songs from day one. Here we go!

The Foundation

Fundamentals that work in every key

Before we head into our first few chords, let's establish a few of the fundamentals. These work in every key and for each chord that you'll learn. You are welcome to come back to this section as often as you need. Some of the information below will help you to develop good habits on the piano and never to develop any of the bad. It's always better to begin something new by establishing good habits rather than needing to break bad ones later.

The parts of your piano or keyboard

First, whether you have a ten-thousand-dollar grand piano, a 1985-upright piano, or a digital keyboard, you're in business to do well with this book. Never assume that because you have a keyboard rather than a *real* piano that your experience is worth any less. We are going to discuss the several parts that make up the piano. Your piano or keyboard will likely have most of them, with the possible exception of foot pedals on cheaper keyboards. Let's talk about each part.

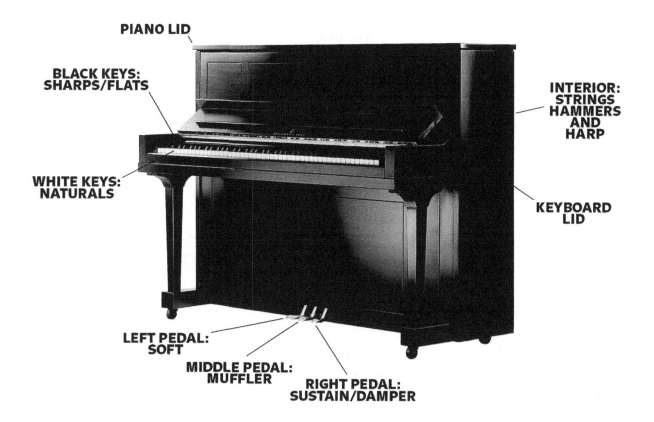

PIANO LID

BLACK KEYS:
SHARPS/FLATS

INTERIOR:
STRINGS
HAMMERS
AND
HARP

WHITE KEYS:
NATURALS

KEYBOARD
LID

LEFT PEDAL:
SOFT

MIDDLE PEDAL:
MUFFLER

RIGHT PEDAL:
SUSTAIN/DAMPER

Piano Lid

The piano lid keeps dust from finding its way to the strings, hammers, and harp. It also dampens the overall sound of an upright piano. Grand pianos also have a lid. It's typically left halfway open. When open, you can hear the hammers strike the strings. Some recording artists like to record the key strike in their records. In the days of synthesized pianos, as on a digital keyboard, hearing the attack of the hammers provides an authentic sound. These sounds are usually sampled along with the actual tones when music companies produce digital piano sounds.

Black Keys: Sharps/Flats

We will talk extensively about black and white keys throughout this book. Black keys are given two names for the same note: sharps (#) and flats (♭). Their technical name is an accidental, which is misleading because you don't play them by accident–or at least you shouldn't. A sharp note raises a note, while a flat lowers it. This makes it seem like they would make two different sounds, but they are given a sharp name in some instances and a flat in others. This will make more sense as you move through this book.

White Keys: Naturals

All white keys are natural notes. This means they have no # or ♭ that follow the letter representing their note name. These tones include C, D, E, F, G, A, and B.

Right Pedal: Sustain/Damper

A standard piano has three pedals found at the bottom of the instrument. The right pedal is known as the sustain or damper pedal. It's the one that you'll use the most. When you strike a note with your fingers while holding down the damper pedal, the note sustains as long as you hold down this pedal with your foot. When you lift your foot, the note stops sounding. If you open up the top of an upright piano while pressing down the damper pedal you'll see all of the string dampers move away from the strings. By depressing the damper pedal, you can play many more notes at one time than you could if you only used your ten fingers. This makes the piano a unique instrument. On a guitar, at most a chord can only contain six notes. You are limited by the number of guitar strings. While it would be unusual, a pianist could use their damper pedal to role a twenty or thirty note chord.

For keyboards, you'll usually only have one pedal and it's the damper/sustain pedal. It plugs into the damper or sustain input on the back of the keyboard. It also may simply be labeled *pedal*. Some cheaper keyboards do not have a damper pedal input. If you own one of these keyboards, I'd recommend saving for a keyboard that has one. You'll use it quite a bit and it makes your playing more enjoyable and much easier.

Middle Pedal: Muffler

The middle pedal is the least used of the piano. It's called a muffler or sostenuto pedal. With it depressed, you can sustain lower selected notes while upper notes remain unaffected by the pedal. I haven't found this pedal to be of much use in pop music. You will typically use the sustain (right) pedal when you perform.

Left Pedal: Soft

The left pedal's technical name is the una corda pedal but is commonly known as the soft pedal. When depressed, it softens the overall volume of the piano and deepens its timbre. Timbre is the tonal character of the sound being played. While this pedal isn't used often, it is nice when you need to play quieter. When I accompany vocalists in a warm-up session I use the soft pedal so that we can hear the pitch of the piano and still hear each other's voices.

Keyboard Lid

Upright and grand pianos come with a lid to cover the keyboard. This keeps dust, debris, and unwanted children and pets from the keys. Be careful that your lid stays up while you play. If it slams down on your hands, you'll wish you had made sure it was secure.

Interior: Strings, Hammers, and Harp

The piano is a stringed instrument that also has a percussive element. Each note on the keyboard has an individual hammer that has a counterpart hammer. They both move when a note is struck. One attacks the string or strings while the other removes the damper allowing the note to be heard. If you get the chance to look inside a piano while it's being played, you'll see a mechanical marvel in action. Lower notes (left side keys) have one thick string per note. Middle notes (middle keys) have two strings per note. Upper notes (right side keys) have three strings per note. In all cases, each string is attached to the harp which is made of heavy metal. If you've ever tried to pick up a piano you know that they're heavy. It's the metal harp that makes it so. The harp is attached to a wooden soundboard that vibrates. This is similar to how an acoustic guitar soundboard vibrates.

Right-hand

The vast majority of people are right-handed. While that may mean that righties have a hand up [get it] on the piano–as melodies and many of the notes on the piano are played with the right-hand–to play well, you'll need both hands to cooperate.

First, we need to assign numbers to each of your fingers on your right-hand. Beginning with your thumb, we count one through five, ending with your pinky. Your thumb is one (R1); index finger is two (R2); middle finger is three (R3); ring finger is four (R4); the pinky finger is five (R5). See the diagram below.

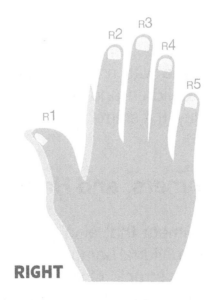

RIGHT

Left-hand

While right-handed people begin with an advantage–initially they are doing more with their dominant hand–left-handed people tend to take gain the advantage as they become more advanced on the piano. Lefties have more dexterity in the hand that performs the root notes for each chord. This means that if you're left-handed, you may naturally be able to place your fingers in more difficult positions than right-handed people.

Notice that your left-hand is the mirrored opposite of your right. If you hold them both in front of your face, you'll see that your thumbs are beside each other and are numbered the same. We begin the left-hand numbering as we did with the right. Your thumb is one (L1); index finger is two (L2); middle finger is three (L3); ring finger is four (L4); the pinky finger is five (L5). See the diagram below.

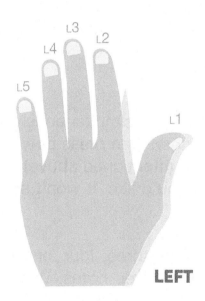

The tennis ball test for good posture

Now that we have your fingers numbered, it's time to sit down at your piano. In my lessons, I keep a tennis ball in the room. For the first lesson, I have my student sit at the piano and place their fingers on the keys. Next, I'll put the tennis ball into the palm of their right and then left-hands. It forces the wrists to stay up while curling the fingers. This is proper form when you play the piano. It doesn't need to be exaggerated and it can change slightly based on what type of chord or melody you are playing, but it is an excellent posture. You'll be able to better stretch your fingers for more difficult chords. Plus, you'll be able to play for longer sessions without needing to take a break because your hands hurt. For some, this will even help if you have arthritis or carpal tunnel. As you progress, you'll learn when this posture is critical and when you can relax it a bit. I recommend beginning with the tennis ball test every time that you sit down to play for the first few weeks. It will help you to establish good habits.

Let's answer a few important questions

So, we are now sitting at the piano and we've made sure we have good posture, it's time to learn a bit about music theory. If you understand these few concepts, they'll be the foundation for every chord and key that you'll play. Since we haven't talked about what a chord or key is yet, let's begin there.

What is a chord?

A chord is multiple notes played simultaneously. This can be as few as two notes or as many as your fingers can press down at one time. In fact, with the addition of the damper pedal (mentioned above), you can hold down every key on the piano at one time if you'd like. It won't sound pleasant, but you could do it.

Most chords are made of two, three, four, or five notes. The chords we will learn in this book are built as three notes. When a single note is played on the piano it is distinct. The ear hears it and knows that it is a single note. The human voice, the trumpet, trombone, snare drum, and flute are among some of the instruments that only play one note at a time. These are called monophonic instruments. Polyphonic instruments include the piano, guitar, bass guitar (even though it's rare to play multiple notes at one time), and the harmonica. They allow more than one note to be performed at a time.

Chords that are made of three notes are called triads. The prefix *tri* means three. Because three notes are played together, our ears cannot easily distinguish the individual notes. Instead, they blend them together to create a rich sound. Chords make for the perfect accompaniment underneath a vocal or lead instrument, like a guitar. You may have heard of one guitarist being called the rhythm player and the other lead. The rhythm player is typically playing chords while the lead player primarily plays single notes.

What is a key and what's a major scale?

I imagine that you've heard of the key of "C" or playing a "C" scale. A key is a group of seven notes, or pitches, that have a unique relationship to one another. This is especially true when played in series, which is known as a scale. For our purposes, we are going to speak about major scales. This means that there is a rule that is followed in every key. As you sit down to play your piano, notice the note in the very middle. It's called *middle C*. It's a white key that is directly before a set of two black keys. See the diagram below.

MIDDLE "C"
-Location On The Piano-

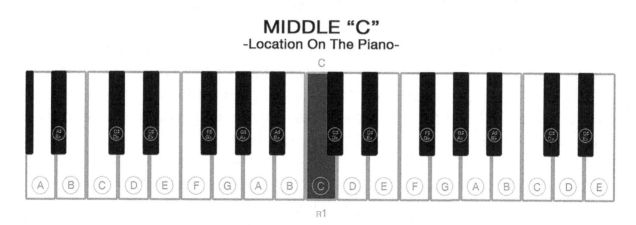

From middle C, we continue up a full step, which means that we skip the half step note, which is a black key in this case. That new note is D. We continue another full step to E. Then, we jump only a half step. There is no black key in between E and F. This means that the half step we need to play is F. Next, we add three more full steps, remembering that half steps are black keys in this case and we are omitting them. The correct notes are G, A, and B. As we continue on, we end up back on a C, but eight notes higher than where we started. That eight note jump is called an octave. The term octave has the prefix oct which means eight. To recap, a major key and the scale we just made began on our foundation note, which is C, and then moved up in this series of jumps: full step, full step, half step, full step, full step, full step, half step. This made the C scale, which is also all of the notes in the key of C Major: C, D, E, F, G, A, B, and C. See the diagram below.

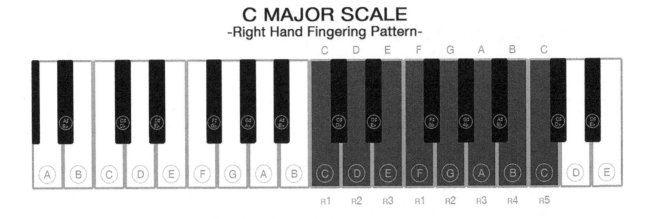

How to play a scale with both of your hands

We've already assigned numbers to our fingers and now know what notes are in a scale. Let's add the two together to talk about which fingers to use when playing the scale. Our hands only have five fingers, but there are eight notes we'd like to play in this scale. At least three fingers are going to be used twice. This is how you play the C scale with the right-hand.

C = R1; D = R2; E = R3 [Then your thumb, R1, moves under your middle finger, R3]; F = R1; G = R2; A = R3; B = R4; C = R5.

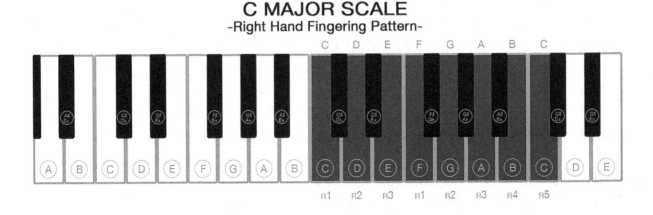

The left-hand pattern is similar to the right, but not exactly the same. While we won't go over left-hand finger position in each key in this book, you can use the following as a template. Please know, some keys require the left-hand to differ slightly from this particular pattern. You should either use your best judgment or refer to the Appendix in the back of this book. This is where I have outlined all major keys with fingering patterns for both hands.

C = L5; D = L4; E = L3; F = L2; G = L1 [Then your middle finger, L3, moves over your thumb, L1] A = L3; B = L2; C = L1.

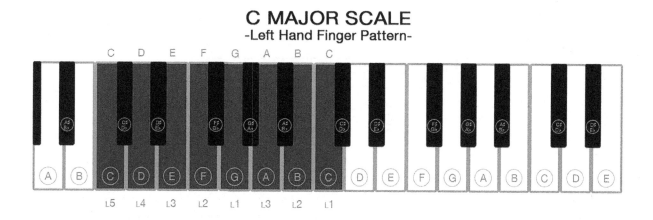

C MAJOR SCALE
-Left Hand Finger Pattern-

Sheet music basics

While I promised you that we weren't going to get into reading sheet music, we have to learn a little bit about it to be prepared to play chords and songs. No, we're not about to lean into Beethoven or Bach. These are the fundamentals that you'll be glad you know. Likely, you've seen some of this before.

Staff, clef, key and time signatures, and measures

Music is laid out on five lines called a staff. Included on the staff are three elements: the clef, key signature, and time signature. The most common two clefs are the treble clef, which looks like a squiggly "G", and the bass clef, which looks like a hook with two dots. While it's not always true, typically the right-hand plays the notes on the treble (upper) clef, while the left plays those on the bass (lower) clef. For our purposes in this book, we will only discuss notes on the treble clef. Melodies are usually written on the treble clef, so you'll be able to play songs using that clef without needing to know the bass clef at this time.

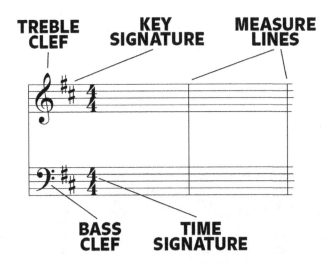

Key and time signatures are variable elements that change per song. Key is flats and sharps written as # and ♭ on their proper note lines. We will discuss several keys. Time signature is written as two numbers. Common time signatures include 4/4, 6/8, and 3/4. You will find vertical lines that separate sections along the staff. These are called measure lines. Like lines on a football field, measure lines make it easy to organize written music and to delineate what's coming next.

Music is built on "4's". In common time, known as 4/4 time–and in which what most pop and worship songs are played–you'll count in repeating sets of four. This means that all note durations in each measure need to total four when you add up all notes held within them. We are getting to that, but let's speak first about notes.

EGBDF and FACE

There are two pneumonic devises that people have used for ages to remember the notes on the treble clef. The first is **Every Good Boy Does Fine** and it stands for each note on the treble clef that is found on a line. It's not the coolest phrase ever, but it is memorable and may be helpful. The other is **F.A.C.E.** The notes in between the lines on the treble clef spell the word *face*. There is no need to come up with a separate pneumonic device in this case. Use both as you memorize the notes on the treble clef. The notes below the staff are C, which has a line through it, and D, which has no line. The two notes above the staff are G, which has no line, and A, that does have a line through it.

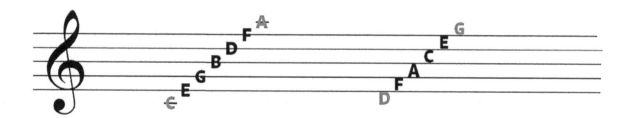

Whole Note and Whole Rest

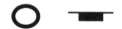

The whole note is represented by a ring with no stem. It's the longest note in common time, being held for four full beats. I tell my younger students that it looks like a tomato. A whole rest also has a four-beat duration. A rest assumes that you will not play anything for the amount of time that is designated by the rest.

Half Note and Half Rest

The half note is held half as many beats as the whole note, thus the name *half*. You hold a half note and half rest for two beats. A half note is represented as a ring with a stem.

Quarter Note and Quarter Rest

A quarter note is held for one-fourth as many beats as the whole note. It is also half of a half note. We're getting confusing now with our math, so I'll stop explaining it that way. Quarter notes are the most common note you'll use early on and are represented by a darkened ring with a stem. A quarter rest is also common and represented by a squiggly line.

Eighth Note and Eighth Rest

The eight note is, you guessed it, held for an eighth of the amount of a whole note. Eighth notes are faster sounding than quarter notes. It takes eight of them to fill a common time measure. They look like a quarter note, but there is an additional flag atop of the stem. The eighth rest also has a flag on top.

Sixteenth Note and Sixteenth Rest

As you have figured out by now, a sixteenth note is held a sixteenth of a whole note. Sixteenth notes are even faster sounding than eighth notes. Sixteenth notes look like eighth notes, but with two flags. A sixteenth rest also has two flags on top.

Tied and Dotted Notes

The final note types that we need to discuss are tied and dotted notes. They both serve similar functions. Tied notes are two notes joined together by a curved line, which is known as a tie. The tie acts to add the two note durations together, equaling one new note duration. A dotted note is similar to a tied note, but a dotted note is always counted as the note duration itself plus half. A dotted note is represented as a note with a small dot beside it.

Let's use an example to understand them both because there are instances when they mean the same thing and others when only one can be used. Let's suppose we tie a quarter note to a half note. This means one beat (the quarter note) is tied together with two beats (the half note). The note being played now totals three beats and is held as long. We can also arrive at this same duration using a dotted note. If we have a dotted half note, the half note is already held two beats plus the addition of one more beat–which is half of the half note. This new note duration is held for three beats.

The two notes differ in that a dotted note cannot be held across a measure line and can only form a few durations. A tied note could technically be held as long as the player would like or until you run out of sheet music to print it upon.

Everything hinges on understanding chord root and inversion positions

Now that we have all of that technical music jargon out of the way, let's get to the fun stuff. All chords have three positions. I tell my students that water has three states: solid, liquid, and gas. In all three states, water's molecular structure is the same. The following is true for chords. Chords have three notes. For our purposes, we are going to speak about a major chord. Later in the book we will cover a few more complex chords.

All major chords are built using the first, third, and fifth notes in the scale with the first note being the root note. As you'll see, you can arrange them in any order you'd like and they'll still add up to the same chord, but in different positions. These new positions are called inversions. Inversions are the lifeblood of the pop/rock/worship keyboardist. They sound amazing and are not hard to play. Soon, you'll be mastering all of your chords in root position and using their inversions.

Root position

When you play any chord with the root note as the lowest note, it's called root position. Some other names for this include, the tonic chord, home base, and even just the chord. Root position assumes that you are playing the first, third, and fifth notes together at one time and in that order. Most people begin by learning all of their chords in root position. While this isn't bad, it's not efficient. Because the piano is a wide instrument, playing all chords in root position means that your hand is flying all over the keyboard to reach chords that are distances apart. We will not only learn our chords in root position, but we will make sure to learn their first and second inversions right away. The benefit of root position is that the tonic (root) note is played on the bottom of the chord and the top note is the fifth of the scale. Every diagram in this book includes the fingering positions for the right-hand that are indicated using an "R" in front of each finger number. Plus, you'll find one root note to be played using the left-hand. Every instance of the left-hand has an "L" beside the finger number. Here is the C chord diagrammed in root position.

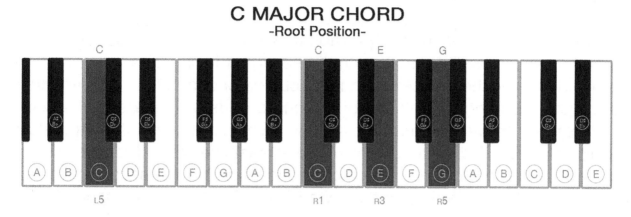

C MAJOR CHORD
-Root Position-

First inversion

When we restructure our chord a little bit we come up with our first inversion. Instead of playing our major chord using the first, third, and fifth notes, we transport the first note above the fifth (it's technically now the eighth note of the scale). Our major chord now reads: third, fifth, and first (again, it's the eighth note of the scale, which an octave repeat of the root note). The benefit of this inversion is that the tonic (root) note is now being played at the top of the chord. For songs with melodies that use the root note quite a bit this inversion is helpful. The downside is that the root note is no longer on the bottom of the chord. In this case, you'll need to supply the root note with your left-hand. Notice that your pinky finger (L5) is still playing the same low C note that it was while playing the C chord in root position. This strengthens the low end of the chord since the inversion has moved the stronger sounding root note, C, to the top of the chord. Here is the C chord diagrammed in its first inversion.

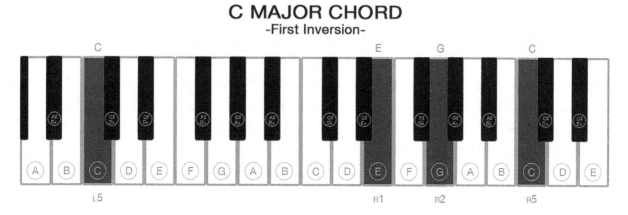

C MAJOR CHORD
-First Inversion-

Second inversion

The second inversion is the last position to learn. What we've rearranged with the first inversion we'll do again with the second. Moving the third note to the top, we now have these notes making up our major chord: fifth, first, and third. Having the third note on the top of the chord adds a richness to the sound being played. As with the first, the second inversion requires the left-hand to play the root note. Notice that there will be at least five notes distance between your left-hand root note and your right-hand chording the second inversion. This spacing can be helpful when you want your chords to sound spaced apart. Here's the C chord using the second inversion. Notice the top note is now E.

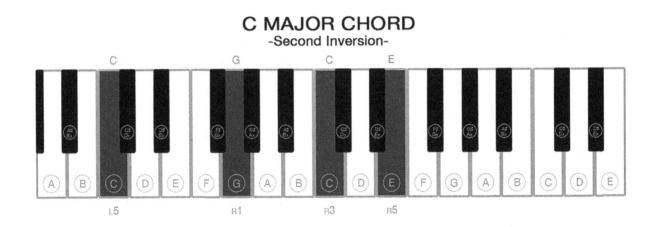

C MAJOR CHORD
-Second Inversion-

Numbers: Music theory at its core

Music is math. While music definitely has an artsy side, at its core, it's math. One plus one always equals two. Even the most unique songs played by the oddest musicians are still performing something that can be quantified. All music follows some rules. Of course, it breaks these rules from time to time too. Known in Nashville, Tennessee as the Nashville Numbers System, all chords live on a chords scale designated by numbers. If you don't live in Nashville, you just call these numbers. You could say this is music theory at its core. Let's discuss what simple music theory is.

Chords scale and how it works in every key

Much like the major scale from the previous section, chords walk up the scale like single notes do. They are as follows: 1, 2m, 1/3, 4, 5, 6m, 5/7, 1. A 1 chord is the tonic chord. This is home base and it sounds like it. Our ears long for a 1 chord. The 2m is the first minor chord we come to. Minor chords are sad sounding counterparts to major chords. The 2m lifts from the 1 chord. The 1/3 chord is the first fractional chord we come to. This means that you have a 1 chord with the third note in the scale shifted up as its bass note. It continues to the lift the progression up. The 4 and 5 chords are our other two major chords along the chords scale. They are definite sounding and easy to hear. A 4 chord is relaxed while a 5 chord is more dominant in nature. They each lift to the 6m. The 6m is the second minor chord along the scale. While the 2m always wants to lift up to the next one–such as a 4 chord or back to a 1–the 6m can stand on its own. It's about as strong to our ears as a 1 chord. The final chord along our chords scale is the 5/7. The same as the 1/3, the 5/7 is a fractional chord. It includes a 5 chord with the seventh note shifted upward as its bass note. Typically, this chord is used as a passing chord, which means that you use it to transition to another chord and won't play it for long durations. This is the basic music theory used for creating and playing pop songs. It may be confusing as just a theory, but will make the most sense as you learn to play these chords on the piano.

The circle of fifths and how this book is laid out.

Before we launch out into the deep of our first key, it may be interesting to note that I haven't laid out this book to go from the keys of C to D then to E and so on. Instead, it's laid out using the circle of fifths. This means that we will learn the key of C which has no sharps or flats–only naturals, or white keys. Our first move is rightward on the circle of fifths wheel (see below), to the key of G, which adds one sharp note (the F# note). Then we'll go back two spaces on the circle to the key of F, which has only one flat note (B♭). This is the only key with flats in it that we'll discuss, but there are several more for future learning. The key of D is next and has two sharp notes (C# and F#). Continuing to add sharps as we go, the following would be the keys of A (3 #'s), E (4 #'s), and B (5 #'s). We will not discuss any further keys in this book but save them for later.

Believe me, if you master each of these, you'll have enough ammunition to play thousands of songs.

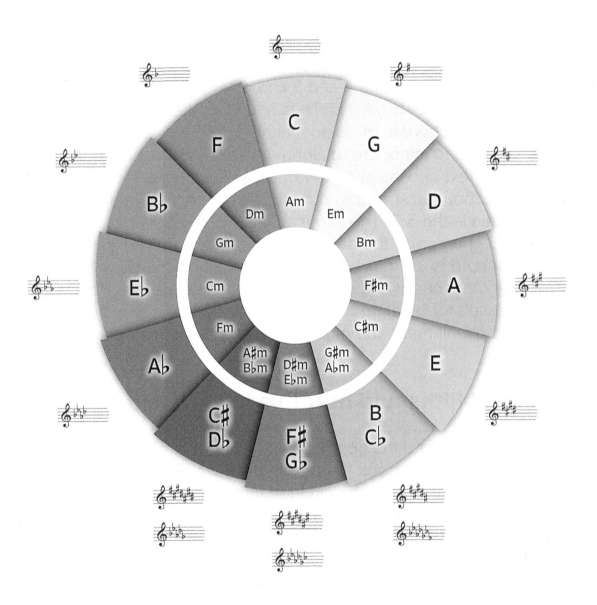

The Key of C

What you need to know about the key of C

The first day of most piano lessons begins by learning the key of C. We usually start there because it's the easiest key in which to play. There are no sharps or flats (black keys). We've used several of the diagrams below in the first section called *The Foundation* so much of this will be familiar to you.

Notes in the key of C and fingering the scale

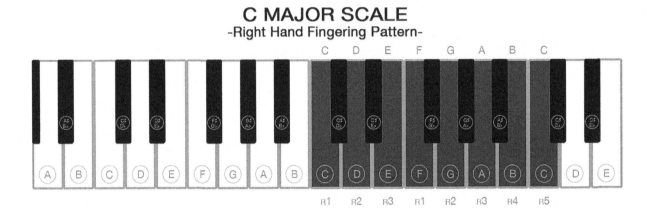

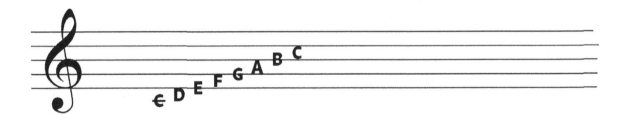

C chord and its inversions

We will not review this in each chapter, but here's a reminder about chords and inversions. In order to be proficient in any key, knowing which chord inversion to use is critical. The following sections teach you the positions using your right-hand to play the C chord and those chords that are related to it. These include all three fingering positions: root position, then first and second inversions. They are equally important. Please be sure you know them well. The C chord in the key of C is the 1 chord. This makes sense as the 1 chord is always built from the root note of the key.

Also, notice that I gave you a single tonic (root) note to play with the left-hand. This stabilizes the chord you are playing by having a lower note played to strengthen the bottom of the chord. While this note isn't required to play the chord, it makes it sound better. With each of these chords, I've recommended that you use the pinky (L5) on your left-hand. It makes for a great starting place for future left-hand usage. However, you are welcome to use any of your left-hand fingers. You could even use a toe if you wanted to be weird.

C MAJOR CHORD
-Root Position-

C MAJOR CHORD
-First Inversion-

C MAJOR CHORD
-Second Inversion-

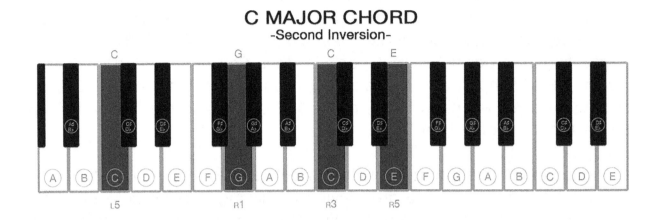

Dm chord and its inversions

The second step up from a C major chord is Dm (pronounced *D minor*). Being only the first chord we come to after the root chord, C, Dm doesn't sound like we have drifted much from home base. It's because we haven't. Dm is the first minor chord we encounter. It sounds sad in comparison with the former major chord, C. You'll notice this distinction in every key when going from the 1 chord to a 2m, or C to Dm in this case.

D MINOR CHORD
-Root Position-

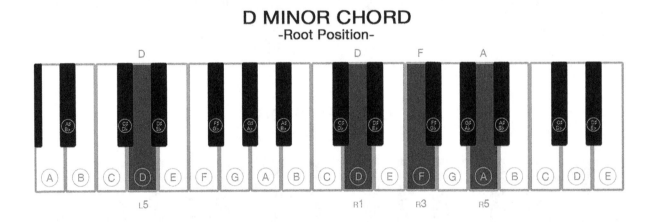

D MINOR CHORD
-First Inversion-

D MINOR CHORD
-Second Inversion-

C/E chord and its inversions

The next stop along the C chord scale is our first fractional chord. Remember, fractional chords are fundamental chords, like the 1 or 5 chord, but with the bass note shifted up. In this case, the bass note has been shifted up two steps from the note C to an E. This gives the chord a lifting sense while keeping the tone happy. Another option for the third chord along this scale would be a 3m chord, or for this key, an Em. The 1/3 is used far more often than a 3m for its upward motion and happier sound. 3m has a darker sound. That's why we'll learn the root position and inversions for the C/E here. However, you will learn the Em chord in the next chapter, so you'll have both options to choose from if you want to hear the difference.

33

C/E MAJOR CHORD
-Root Position-

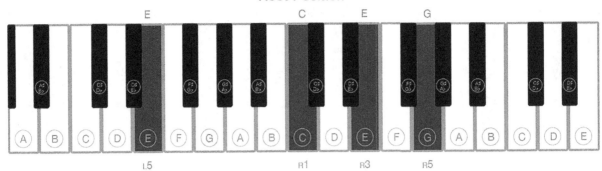

C/E MAJOR CHORD
-First Inversion-

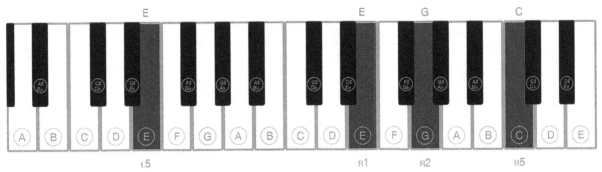

C/E MAJOR CHORD
-Second Inversion-

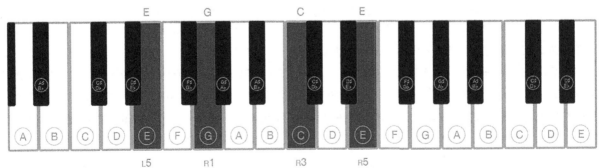

F chord and its inversions

The F chord is the fourth chord along the scale. It's the second of the three fundamental chords (1, **4**, and 5). You'll notice that the notes that make up an F are almost identical those of a Dm. This will come in handy as you learn to transition from chord to chord. The difference between a Dm and an F is that we've replaced the D note with a C. A 4 chord, or F in this case, feels like it rises up from the 1 chord. It's almost unsettled until it moves back to 1. If you play a 1 chord, or C, and then move to the 4, F, you'll hear what I mean. Here's how to play all three versions of F.

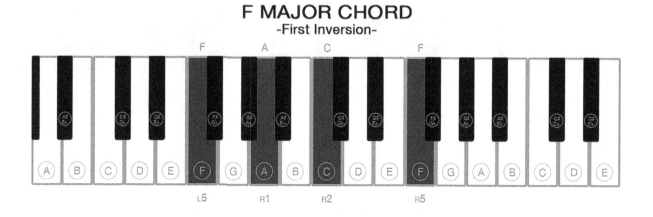

35

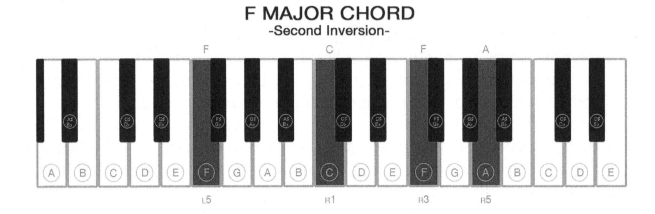

F MAJOR CHORD
-Second Inversion-

G chord and its inversions

G is the 5 chord in our series. The 5 chord is dominant. It doesn't sound like any other chord along the chord scale. It's often referred to as the dominant fifth. To the ear, it longs to move forward to a 1 chord or back to a 4. If you were to end a song on a 5, it would feel incomplete. Here's how to play the 5 chord, G.

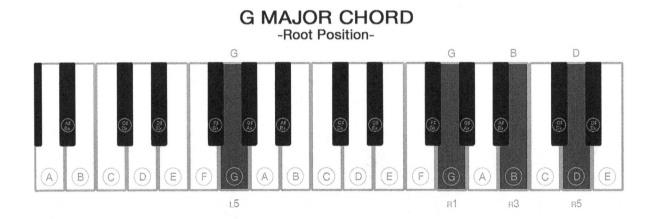

G MAJOR CHORD
-Root Position-

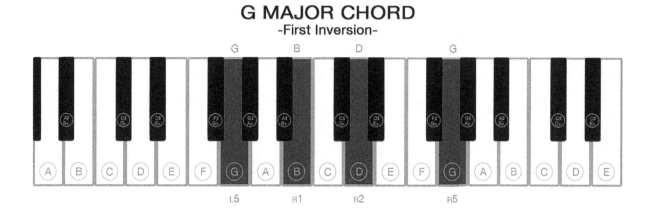

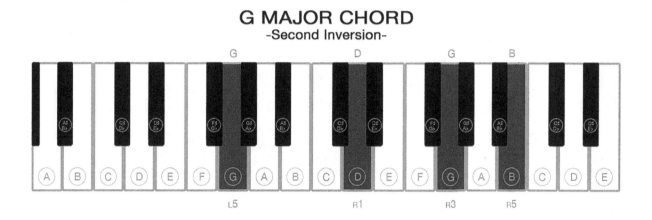

Am chord and its inversions

The 6m is the most dominant sounding minor chord you can play. It shares two of the same notes with the 1 chord, so you can imagine why it's so powerful. Songs often begin on a 6m rather than a 1 because it's more dramatic to the ear. The Am is the 6m in the key of C.

A MINOR CHORD
-Root Position-

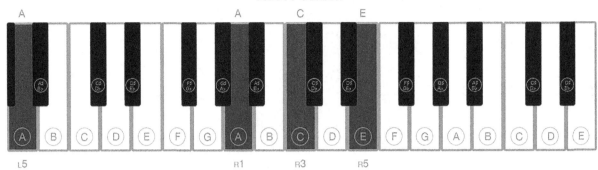

A MINOR CHORD
-First Inversion-

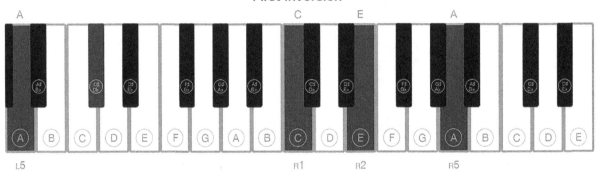

A MINOR CHORD
-Second Inversion-

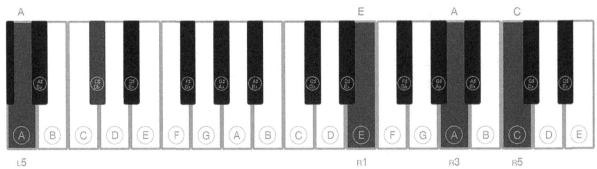

G/B chord and its inversions

The last chord we'll learn in this key is the 5/7, or G/B. Built from a 5 chord, G, the bass note is shifted up two full steps, making it a 7 note, or B. If you play Am to G/B, you'll hear the lifting nature of the G/B. It's another chord that would be strange on which to end a song. Here's how to play your root position and inversions of G/B.

39

Practice progressions

It's time for some practice measures (you could even call these songs if you are feeling spunky). Take your time learning them. You are welcome to use a metronome with a slower BPM (beats per minute) such as 55BPM. A metronome is a musician's best friend and most hated foe. Even if you aren't familiar with the word, you've likely heard the in-time clicks of a metronome coming from somewhere. Metronomes provide a series of clicks or ticks that are programmed to a selected rate. 50-90 beats per minute would be fairly slow, while 90-150BPM would be rather fast. If you do not own a metronome, you can download several metronome apps for free to your smartphone, tablet, or computer.

Playing chords in root position

Now, let's move on to the good stuff. If you play each of these chord series solely in root position, you'll be sounding great, but playing inefficiently. Let's begin by only using root position and then we'll put our inversions to the test.

Chord patterns using root position

The following three rhythm examples are some of the most popular chord patterns that you'll find. You may even find them in some of your favorite songs. The first pattern is likely the most famous: 1, 5, 6m, 4. While you play it, see if you can recognize it as the chord pattern for one of your favorite tunes. We will use all three of these chord patterns throughout the rest of this book. The only thing that should change is the key in which you are playing. Hopefully, this will help you make a connection between chords, numbers, keys, and how they all integrate together.

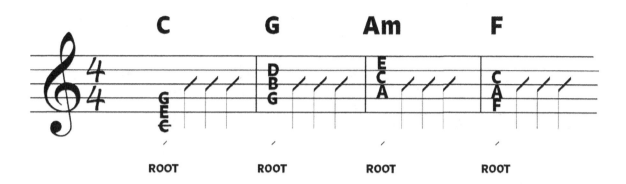

The next pattern does not begin with a 1 chord. However, it is still in the key of C. The first chord in a song does not determine the key. It's the number of flat or sharp notes determines the key. Since there are no flats or sharps in this one, we are still in the key of C. This pattern is 2m, 1, 6m, 5.

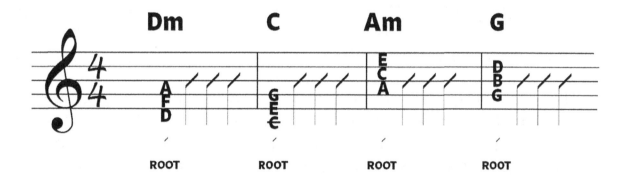

The final progression that we will go over in each chapter is 1, 4, 5, 6m. There are thousands of more progressions you could play. We are learning a few of the most common and using the same ones in each chapter so that we notice continuity. As you play this one you may find that as each chord moves to the next it feels like it is moving upward. There is a lifting motion to this pattern.

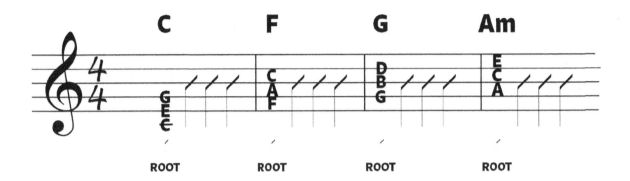

Let's use our inversions

Now it's time to put some of our inversions to good use. As you played the chords solely in root position, hopefully you've noticed how much your right-hand had to move across the keys. For some of the progressions, your right-hand moved more than a foot. As you'll see next, inversions, used in the right shape, make transitioning chords easier. They also sound more connected because the notes are closer together.

One of the best ways to train your hands to stay within inversion boundaries is to set up a few bumpers. In the diagram below, I've placed pencils on the lower B and upper C keys. These act like bumpers in a bowling alley or lines on a road that keep you safe as you drive a car. While these aren't required, I recommend using them as you learn how to shape your fingers for each progression. I know they have helped all of my students perform at a higher level.

CHORDS BETWEEN C AND B
-Pencils on B and C Notes-

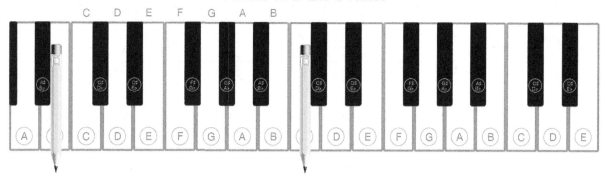

Finally, all of the patterns that are shown are transcribed for your right-hand only. It's assumed that you will play the root note with your left-hand as well. This means that for the first progression, C, G, Am, F, your left-hand should play the notes: C, G, A, and F. While I recommend using your pinky finger, L5, of your left-hand, try a few of these using other fingers as well.

Playing all chords between notes C and B using root position and inversions

The first series keeps the 1 chord in root position while most of the others require inversions to stay within our boundary marker pencils. Don't forget to use your left-hand as well. It should play the root note of each of these chords.

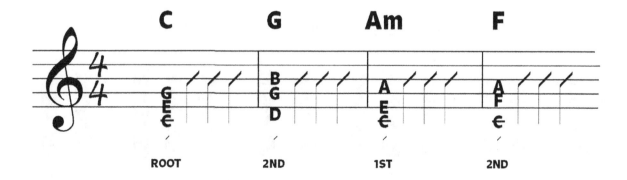

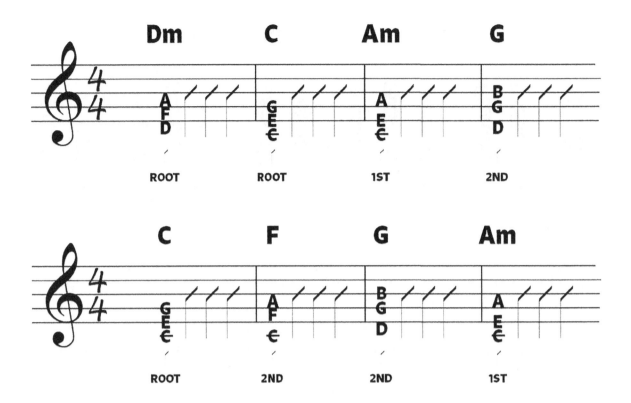

Playing all chords between notes E and D using root position and inversions

Let's move our pencils from the B note up two to the D and move the C pencil up two to an E. View the diagram below and then try to play the patterns using our new sets of inversions.

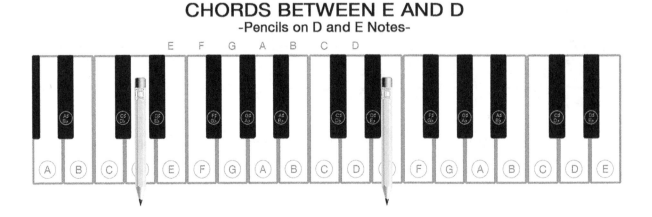

CHORDS BETWEEN E AND D
-Pencils on D and E Notes-

Playing all chords between notes G and F using root position and inversions

In our final set of patterns in this chapter, move your pencils up one more time. Now, place pencils on the F and G notes. These progressions are the same as before but staying between these new note sets.

CHORDS BETWEEN G AND F
-Pencils on F and G Notes-

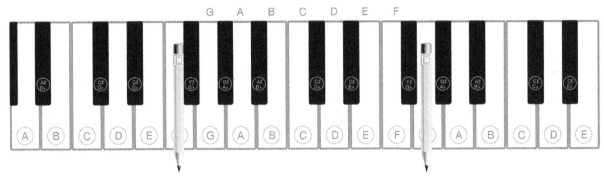

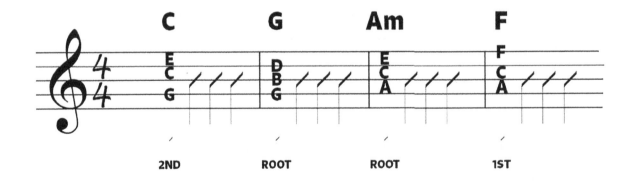

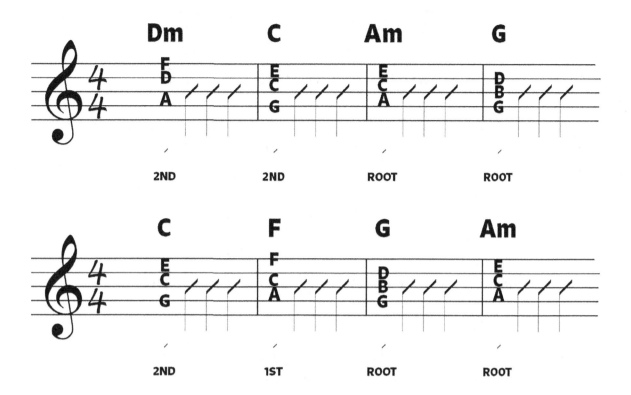

Before we move on to the key of G that's next, the three patterns above are common, but are hardly the only ones you can use. In fact, we haven't even used the C/E or G/B chords. You could replace any of the C or G chords in the previous progressions with our fractional versions. As you learn some of your favorite songs, you may find some of these progressions are those songs' backbones. Now, onward!

The Key of G

What you need to know about the key of G

The key of G is the first tick to the right on the circle of fifths wheel, which you learned about in the first chapter, *The Foundation*. This means that we exchange the natural note, F, for the black key, F# (Pronounced *F sharp*). Because there is only one sharp, it's only slightly more difficult than the key of C. As we move along adding sharps, the difficulty level increases. Don't let that slow you down. Each key has its own unique sound and is worth learning.

Notes in the key of G and fingering the scale

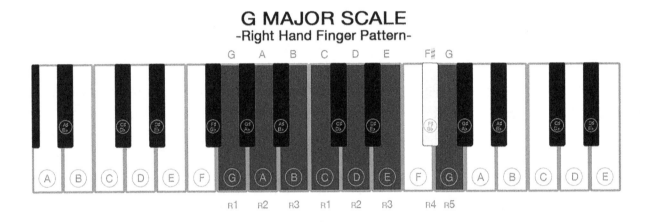

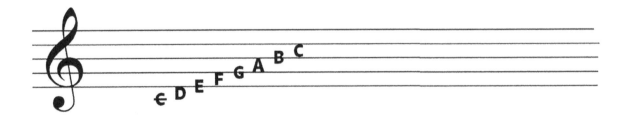

G chord and its inversions

As with the key of C, the 1 chord is always the root chord and, in this case, it's a G. Also the same as C, the G chord has no flats or sharps to play. Its root position and first and second inversions feel identical to many of those from the previous key. G, which is now the 1 chord, is the same chord that you learned in the previous key of C as the 5. Here's a reminder of how to play each of those G chords.

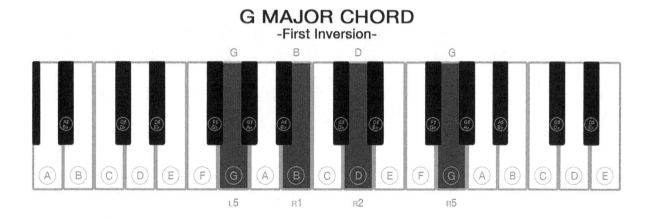

49

G MAJOR CHORD
-Second Inversion-

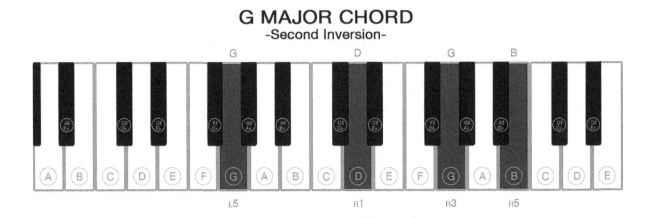

Am chord and its inversions

Moving up, the 2m for the key of G is Am. You played this chord in the key of C, but it was the 6m for that key. Notice that many keys are related and share some of the same chords.

A MINOR CHORD
-Root Position-

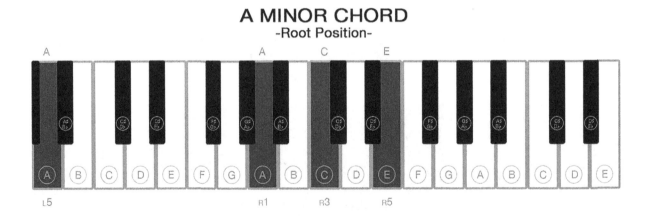

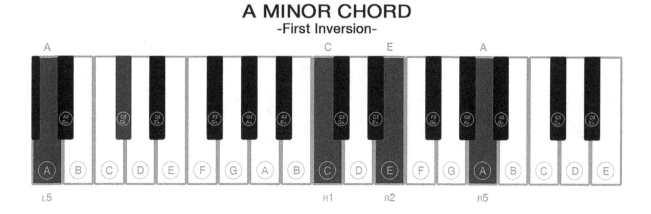

A MINOR CHORD
-First Inversion-

A MINOR CHORD
-Second Inversion-

G/B chord and its inversions

The 1/3 chord is G/B. Play this one the same way you did when you played the 1 chord, G, but move your left-hand from a G note to a B. While the inversions are the exact same, I've created the fingering diagrams for this chord to begin an octave (eight notes) lower for the right-hand. The lowered octave may make it seem like it's in a different chord series, but the G and G/B play the same way. The only difference will be the up-shifted bass note.

G/B MAJOR CHORD
-Root Position-

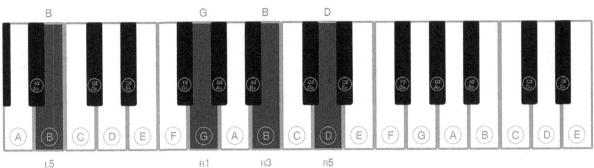

G/B MAJOR CHORD
-First Inversion-

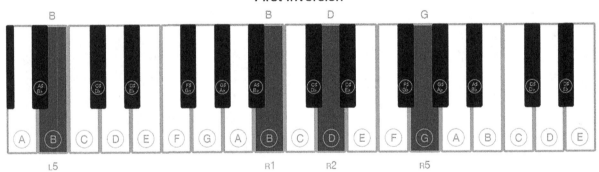

G/B MAJOR CHORD
-Second Inversion-

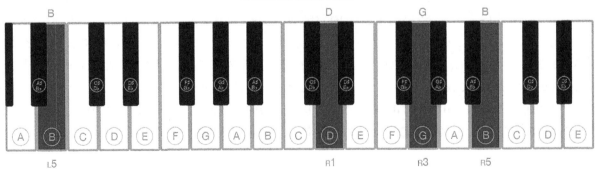

C chord and its inversions

The 4 chord in the key of G is C. We learned C as our first chord in the last chapter. Play these inversions the same may that you did previously. You can try using different right-hand fingers if you'd like to play something new. For instance, play the root chord using R1, R2, and R4. Doing so leaves your R5 (pinky finger) to play an additional A or B note down the road, which would make the chord a C6 or CMaj7. We will discuss chord suffixes, like 6 and Maj7 chords, as part of this series of books.

C MAJOR CHORD
-Root Position-

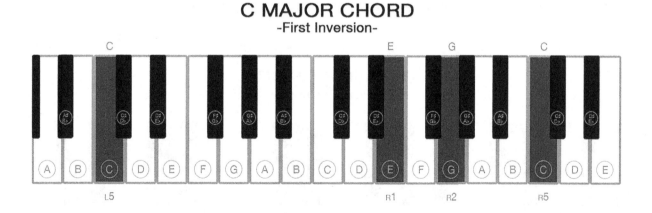

C MAJOR CHORD
-First Inversion-

C MAJOR CHORD
-Second Inversion-

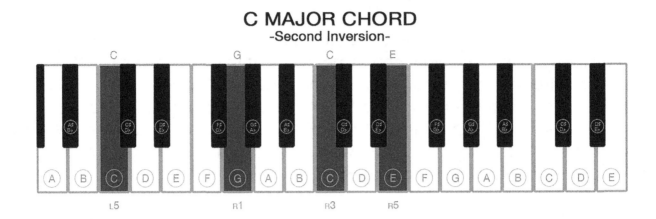

D chord and its inversions

The 5 chord is D. Remember, there is strength in a 5 chord. It also always sounds like it wants to go somewhere. It could be that it wants to go back to a 1, or G in this key, or it could fall back to a 4, which is C. The D chord is the first that we encounter with a sharp note, F#. To add sharps, you may need to move your wrist up to accommodate the required stretch. This means that your R3 (middle finger) should help draw your entire hand closer to the top of the keyboard. Your R1 (thumb) and R5 (pinky) will need to move up too. If this is an awkward stretch at first, practice it several times. Take your hand on and off the D chord until it feels natural. Here's how to play all three versions of D.

D MAJOR CHORD
-Root Position-

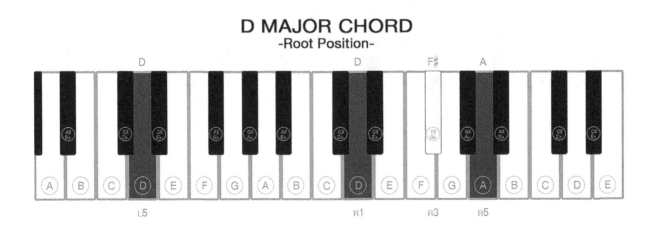

D MAJOR CHORD
-First Inversion-

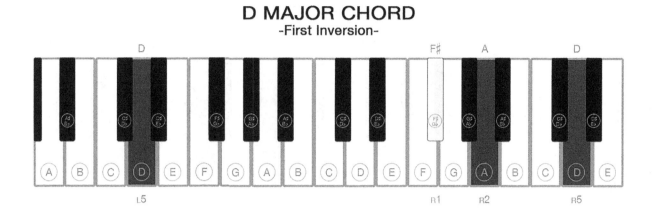

D MAJOR CHORD
-Second Inversion-

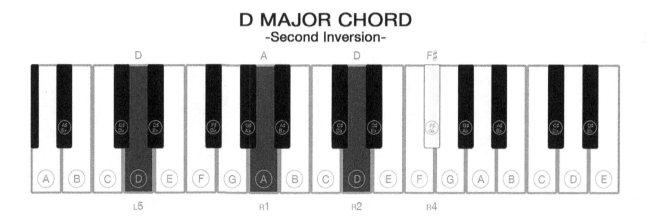

Em chord and its inversions

The Em is the 6m chord. We are back to playing chords with no black keys again. The Em is simple in comparison to D. In the previous chapter, I mentioned that the Em chord could be played as the 3m chord in the key of C, rather than using the 1/3, or C/E. This is that chord. Here's how to play an Em chord and all of its variations.

E MINOR CHORD
-Root Position-

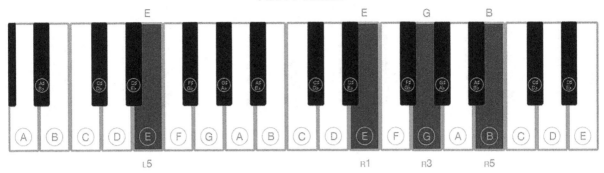

E MINOR CHORD
-First Inversion-

E MINOR CHORD
-Second Inversion-

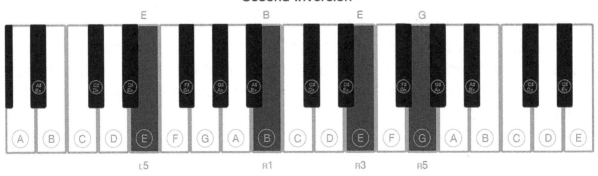

D/F# chord and its inversions

The last chord in the key of G is the 5/7, or D/F#. D and D/F# are identical, only the bass note shifts up from D to F#. Here are all three versions.

D/F# MAJOR CHORD
-Root Position-

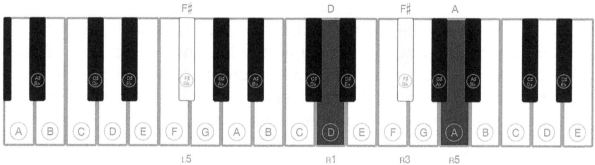

D/F# MAJOR CHORD
-First Inversion-

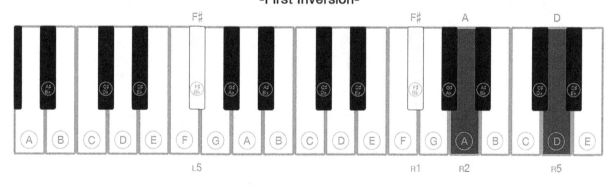

D/F# MAJOR CHORD
-Second Inversion-

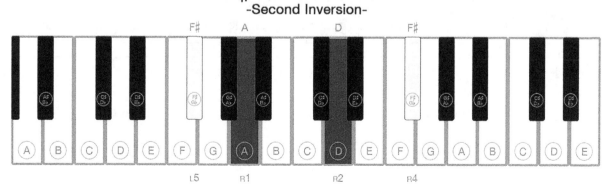

57

Practice progressions

It's time for some practice measures. As before, you could even call these songs. Take your time learning them. Use a metronome with a slower BPM (beats per minute) such as 60 or 70BPM.

Playing chords in root position

Here are all of your progressions with each chord played in root position. You should notice that they sound very similar to the ones you played in the key of C because they are same numbered progressions. For instance, the first progression is still 1, 5, 6m, 4. The difference is that you are now playing in the key of G and you've added an F# note in place of the F natural.

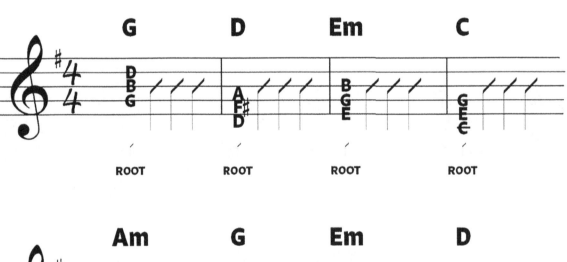

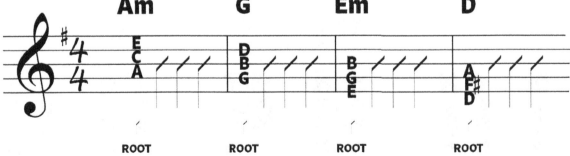

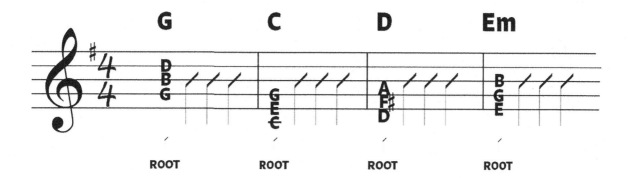

Playing all chords between notes G and F♯

As with the previous chapter, let's use pencils (or whatever bumper you have) as makeshift guardrails keeping us inside our inversion spacing. Let them act like a force field or an electric fence that you don't want to get close to. First, we'll begin by placing our pencils on the lower F♯ and upper G notes which will help us stay between the lower G and upper F♯ notes. We're using the same progressions that are above, only with the appropriate inversions. If you find your first pencil teetering because of the black key being raised, angle the pencil so that it has more stability against the key.

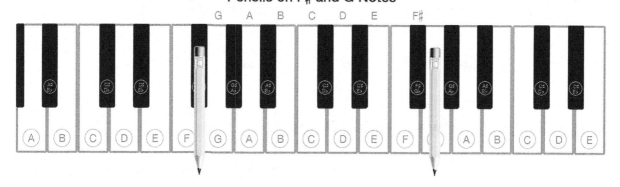

Micah Brooks

Playing all chords between notes B and A

For our second set, move your pencils up to the A and B notes. This should keep all of your chords between the B and A notes on your piano.

60

CHORDS BETWEEN B AND A
-Pencils on A and B Notes-

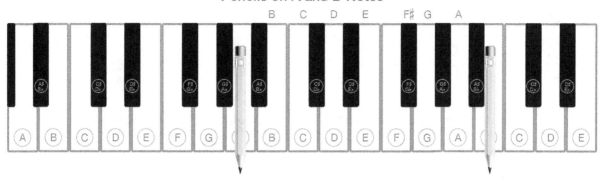

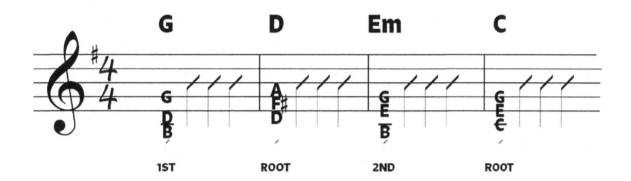

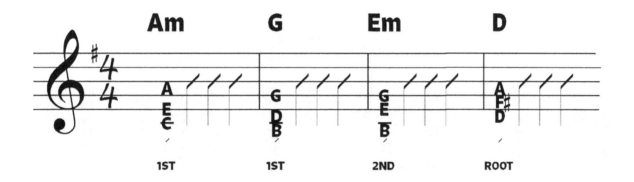

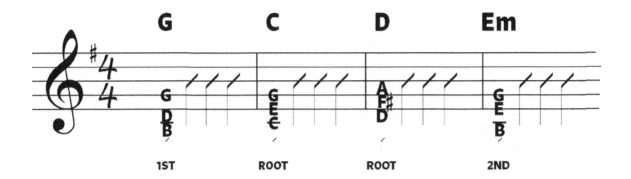

Playing all chords between notes D and C

Last, move your pencils up to the C and D notes. This final set keeps your right-hand fingers between D and C. As an aside, this set uses the second inversion of the G chord. This means that a B note is on the top of the chord each time you play the G. The B note is the third note in the G scale. The third note of the scale is known as the color note of the chord. It's the note that adds the most definition to the chord. As you play through these progressions, notice each time you play the G chord in its second inversion. There is a rich sound playing from the top of the chord because of that third note, B, that's up there.

CHORDS BETWEEN D AND C
-Pencils on C and D Notes-

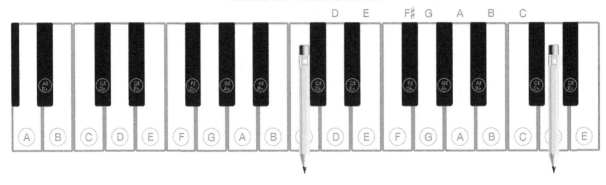

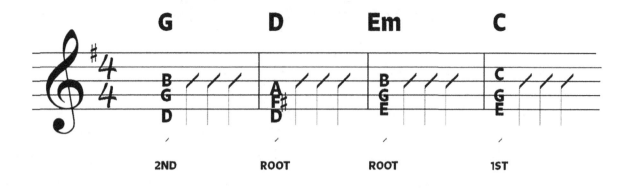

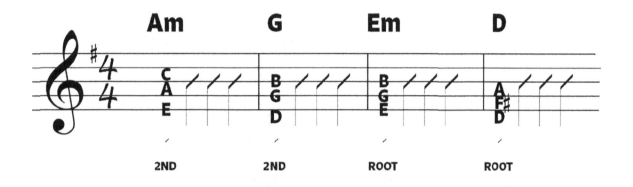

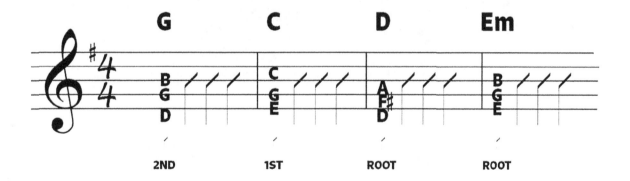

The Key of F

What you need to know about the key of F

Moving one tick to the left on the circle of fifths from C, we find the key of F. This is two ticks left from the key of G. While this is the only key with flat notes (♭) that we will learn in this book, it's as easy as the key of G. There is only one flat note: B♭. This means it plays as easily as the key of C, except for the single black key, B♭. B♭ is replacing B natural, making this the key of F.

Notes in the key of F and fingering the scale

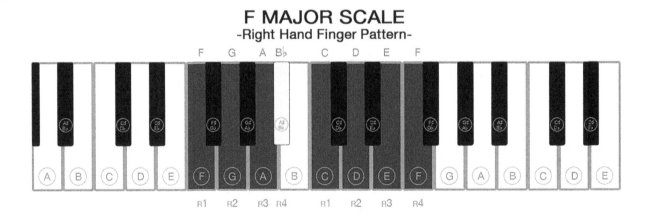

F MAJOR SCALE
-Right Hand Finger Pattern-

F chord and its inversions

By now you've probably figured out what each of the chords along the numbers scale should be. That being said, the key of F begins with the 1 chord, F. Here's how to play the F chord. It is the exact same as you learned in the first chapter when you learned the 4 chord in the key of C, which is also F.

F MAJOR CHORD
-Root Position-

F MAJOR CHORD
-First Inversion-

F MAJOR CHORD
-Second Inversion-

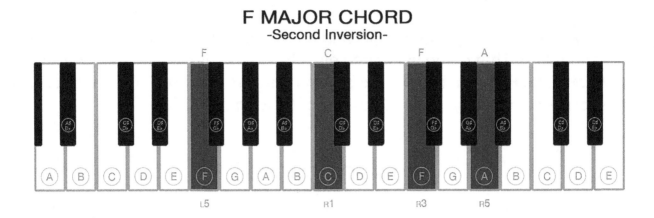

Gm chord and its inversions

The 2m chord is Gm. Your right-hand will need to stretch to include the B♭ note in each position of this chord. I recommend using the fingers suggested, but you can use whichever finger works best for you. Younger players with smaller hands should consider using your middle (R3) and pinky (R5) fingers to make the stretches. The goal is to be able to play the chord with any finger that works best for you. These fingerings are the way that I naturally play them. Here's how to play each of the positions for Gm.

G MINOR CHORD
-Root Position-

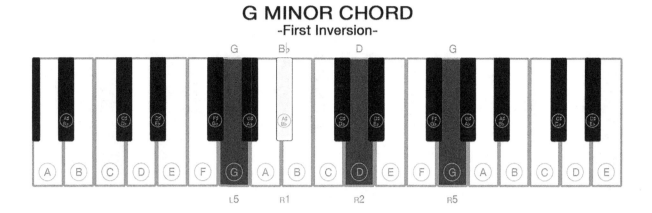

F/A chord and its inversions

The 1/3 chord is F/A. You build it exactly as you have with the 1 chord, F, only move your left-hand from the root note, F, up to the third note of the scale, which is A. Finger an F/A using the following diagrams.

F/A MAJOR CHORD
-Root Position-

F/A MAJOR CHORD
-First Inversion-

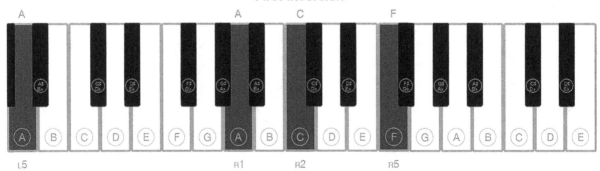

F/A MAJOR CHORD
-Second Inversion-

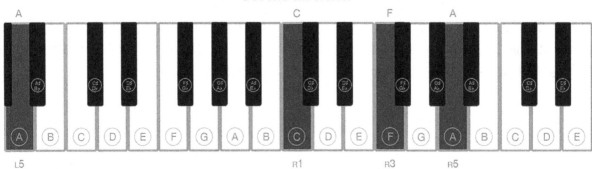

B♭ chord and its inversions

Now let's move to the 4 chord, B♭. This is the only flat chord we will learn in this book, but there are several more you could learn down the road. The B♭ chord and Gm finger nearly the same, except that the G note in each of your Gm chords has been moved to an F in each of these B♭ chords. Here's how to play them.

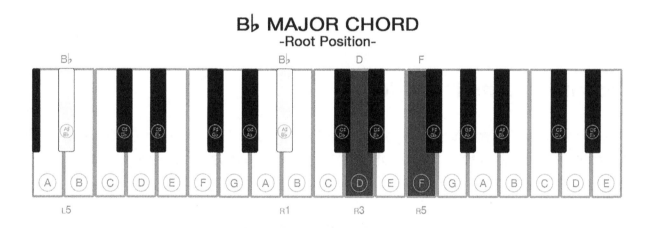

B♭ MAJOR CHORD
-Root Position-

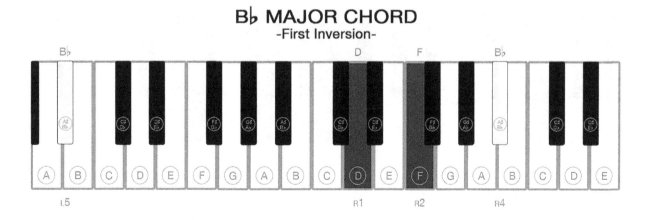

B♭ MAJOR CHORD
-First Inversion-

B♭ MAJOR CHORD
-Second Inversion-

C chord and its inversions

The 5 chord is C. You've now played a C chord in the keys of C, G, and F. The inversions are the same for all of them, so you're ahead of the game.

C MAJOR CHORD
-Root Position-

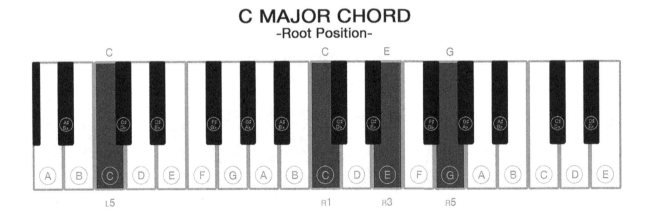

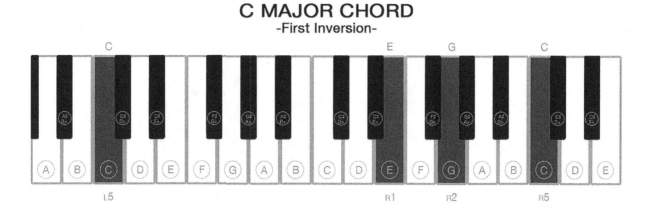

Dm chord and its inversions

The 6m chord is Dm. There are no flat notes to play in this chord, so it's as easy as a C or F chord. A Dm and an F chord are nearly the same set of notes, except that the C note in an F chord has been raised to a D note in the Dm. Here's how to play all three Dm chords. You also learned this chord in the first chapter, *The Key of C*.

D MINOR CHORD
-Root Position-

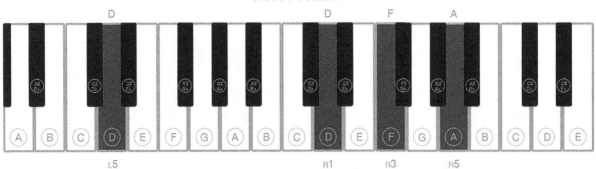

D MINOR CHORD
-First Inversion-

D MINOR CHORD
-Second Inversion-

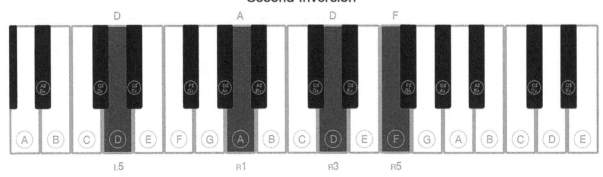

C/E chord and its inversions

The 5/7 chord, or C/E, is the final chord for this key. The C/E is simple. Make sure to raise your root note from a C to an E. You should experiment using other fingers on your left-hand to play the E. Perhaps use your pinky finger (L5) to play a normal C chord and then switch to your middle finger (L3) to then play the E note. It should make the chord feel like it is audibly lifting upward. Here's how to play them.

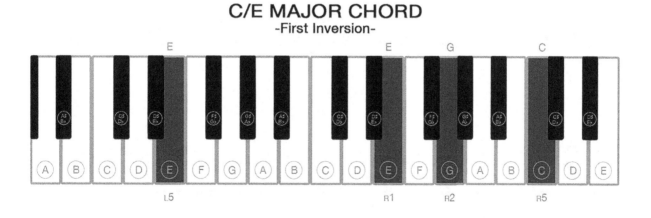

C/E MAJOR CHORD
-Second Inversion-

Practice progressions

Let's try some of our practice progressions again, but using our new key of F. You'll need your pencils or bumpers that you used earlier. The only difference between the keys of C and G you'll likely notice is how awkward it is to include the B♭ note instead of the simple B natural note. Over time, F will likely be one of your favorite keys. Initially, it may be tough to include that one flat note. Practice will certainly make perfect.

Playing chords in root position

Our first set of chords are each in root position. Your hand will be flying all over your keyboard. While it may sound beautiful, it's not efficient. We'll get into the inversions next.

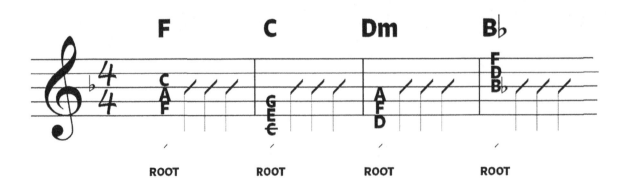

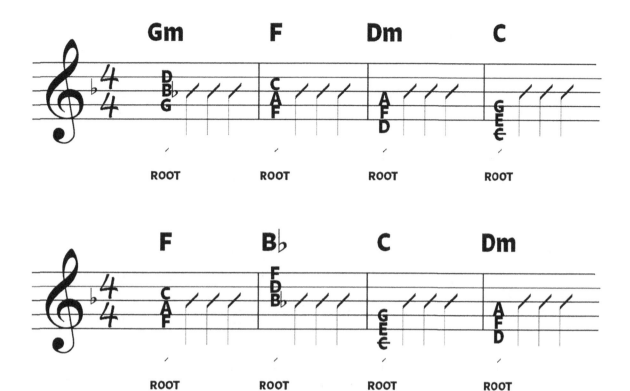

Playing all chords between notes F and E

Bring out your trusty pencils, or your bumper of choice, and place them on the E and F notes. This should keep each of your chords between the F and E notes. This also keeps each of your 1 chords in root position.

CHORDS BETWEEN F AND E
-Pencils on E and F Notes-

75

Playing all chords between notes A and G

Now, move your pencils up two notes each. They should be on the notes G and A. This set of inversions keeps all notes between A and G. This first inversion of the F chord is used in each of these.

CHORDS BETWEEN A AND G
-Pencils on G and A Notes-

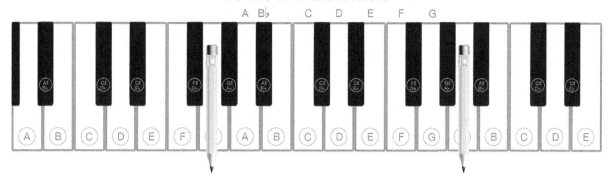

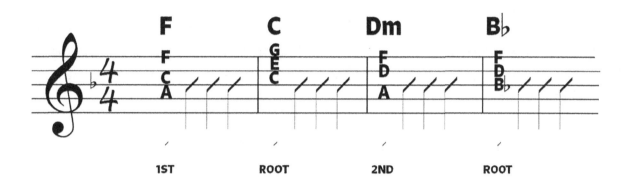

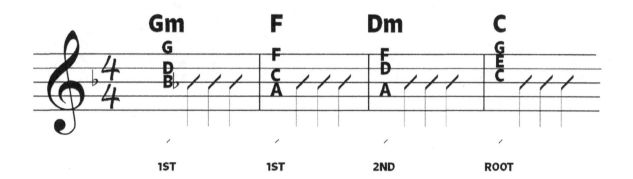

77

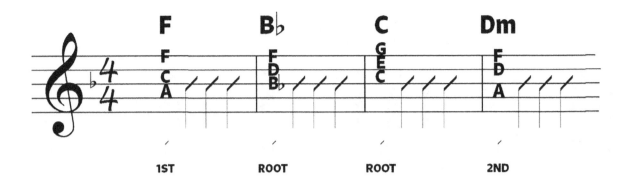

| 1ST | ROOT | ROOT | 2ND |

Playing all chords between notes C and B♭

Last, move your pencils up two more notes. This time you'll have pencils on B♭ and C. You may need to angle your pencil so that it stays on the B♭ note since it's raised to reach the black key. This final set makes your F chords fall in the second inversion.

CHORDS BETWEEN C AND B♭
-Pencils on B♭ and C Notes-

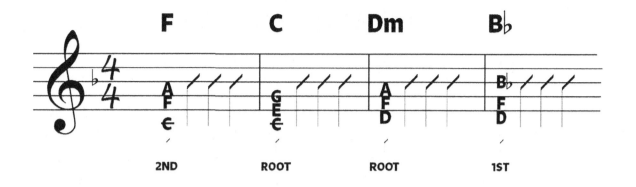

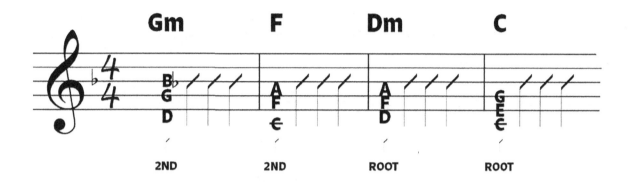

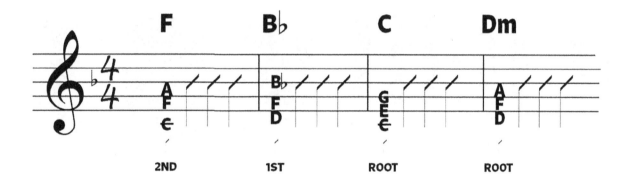

The Key of D

What you need to know about the key of D

The key of D is two ticks to the right on the circle of fifths wheel. The key of G included the F# note. Now, we add the C# note to the F# which gives us the notes in the key of D. Guitar players tend to enjoy playing in this key, so there are thousands of songs in it. You'll likely find several of your favorite tunes in this one. While there is plenty of physical space between the notes E and F#, there is less between C# and D. This makes transitioning to chords that include one or the other note slightly more difficult. As we've discussed up to this point, practice makes perfect.

Notes in the key of D and fingering the scale

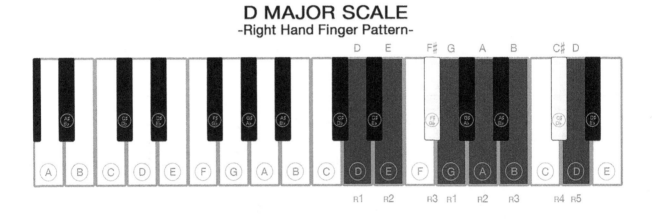

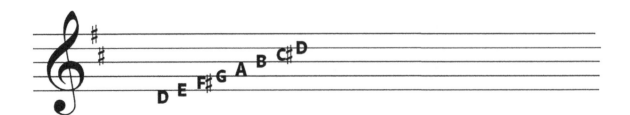

D chord and its inversions

The key of D begins with the D chord. As with the chords B♭ and the Gm you learned in the last chapter, some of these chords require some finger stretches. If you find yourself struggling, take a break and come back to them the next day. Sometimes overdoing it can lead to the law of diminishing returns. This is when you practice and practice yet make little forward progress. We want to avoid this as much as possible. Here are three shapes for the D chord.

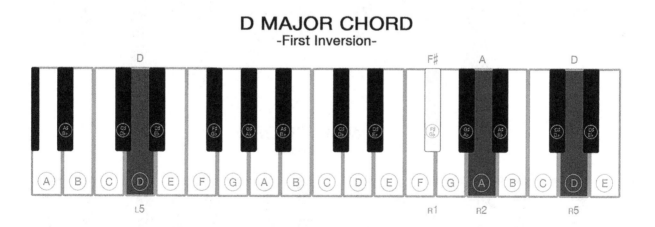

D MAJOR CHORD
-Second Inversion-

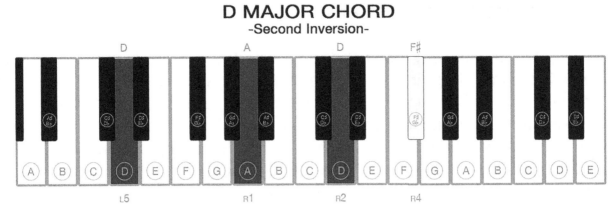

Em chord and its inversions

The 2m chord in the key of D is Em. This is the same Em that you found as the 6m in the key of G and that you could use as the 3m in the key of C. Here are each of the positions for Em.

E MINOR CHORD
-Root Position-

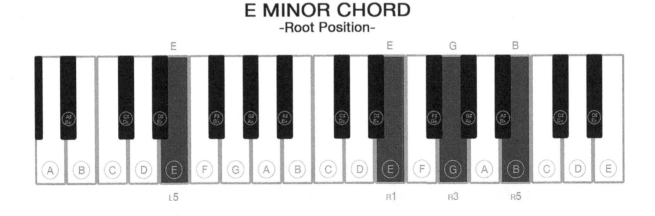

E MINOR CHORD
-First Inversion-

E MINOR CHORD
-Second Inversion-

D/F♯ chord and its inversions

D/F♯ is the 1/3 in the key of D. It's the same as the 5/7 that you played in the key of G.

D/F♯ MAJOR CHORD
-Root Position-

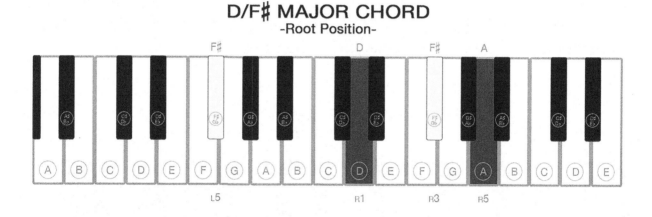

D/F♯ MAJOR CHORD
-First Inversion-

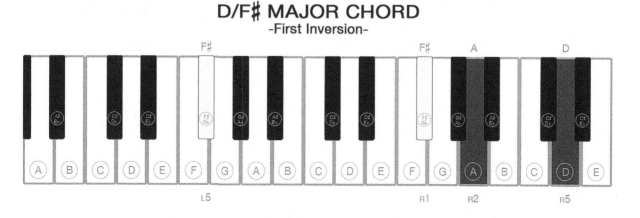

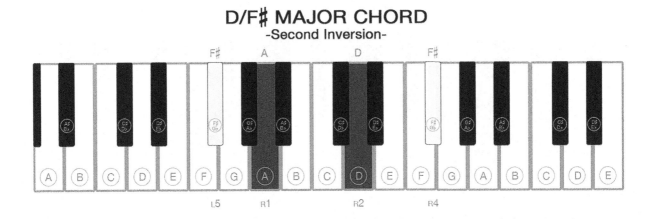

G chord and its inversions

The key of D's 4 chord is G. This is the third time you're seeing this one. First in the key of C as its 5, then as the 1 chord in the key of G, and now as the 4 chord in the key of D. I imagine you are beginning to master this one. Here are the positions you need just in case you'd like the reference.

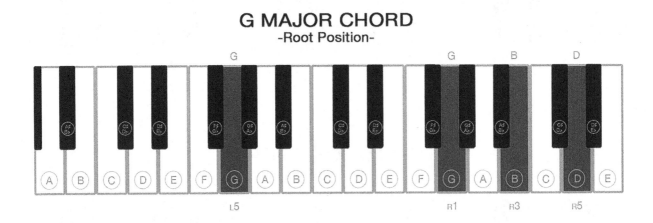

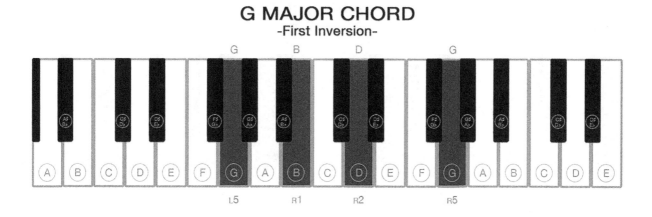

G MAJOR CHORD
-First Inversion-

G MAJOR CHORD
-Second Inversion-

A chord and its inversions

The 5 chord is an A major. You'll finger this chord similar to how you did the D chord. If you find any of these positions difficult, practice taking your hand on and off the piano until your fingers fall into place naturally. Here are the three positions for A. You'll need them for the following two chapters as well.

A MAJOR CHORD
-Root Position-

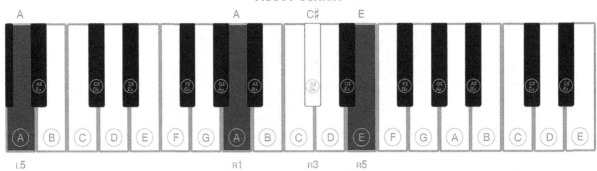

A MAJOR CHORD
-First Inversion-

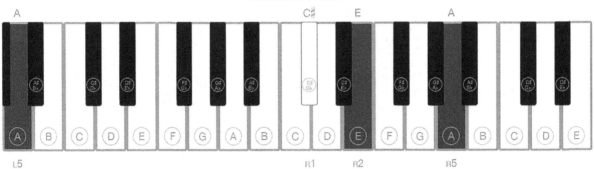

A MAJOR CHORD
-Second Inversion-

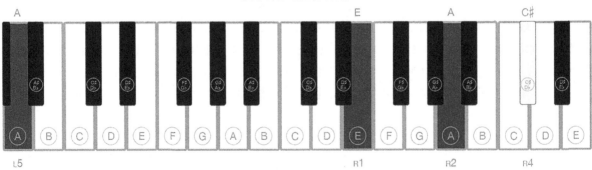

Bm chord and its inversions

The 6m for the key of D is Bm. Notice that all three positions of the Bm look nearly the same as the D chord positions, but the A note has been moved up to a B. Here's how to play Bm. This is a chord in which you may want to experiment with different fingers. The ones that I recommend work well, but if your hand is smaller you could replace all your ring finger (R4) positions with your pinky (R5).

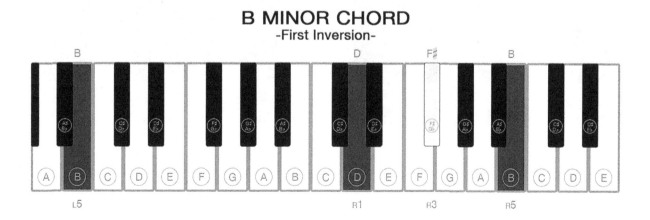

B MINOR CHORD
-Root Position-

B MINOR CHORD
-First Inversion-

B MINOR CHORD
-Second Inversion-

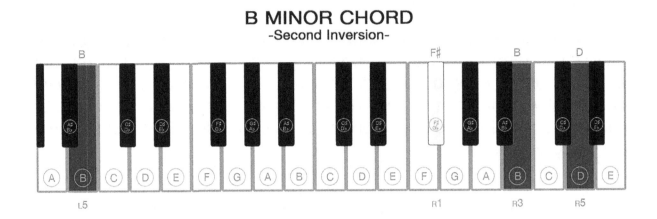

A/C# chord and its inversions

The 5/7 is A/C#. It's just as you played the A chord, but now move your left-hand root note from an A to a C#.

A/C# MAJOR CHORD
-Root Position-

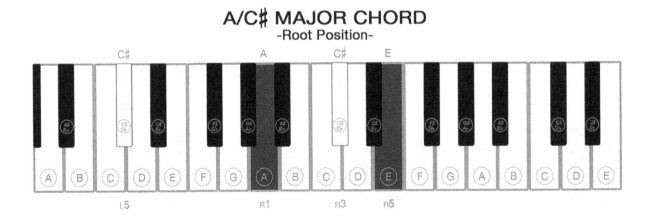

A/C♯ MAJOR CHORD
-First Inversion-

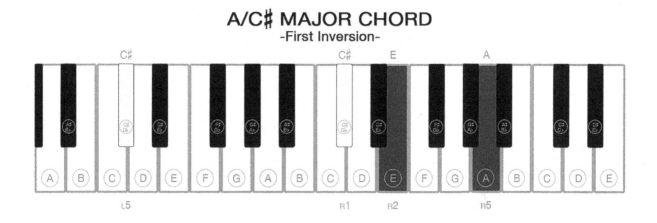

A/C♯ MAJOR CHORD
-Second Inversion-

Practice progressions

Our practice progressions are next. Instead of playing these at a slower pace, like 55BPM (beats per minute), speed your metronome up to 90BPM. This means that you'll make your transitions faster. 90BPM is considered mid-tempo, while 55BPM is considered slow. You could also split the measures. This means that you strike each chord twice per measure then move the next chord rather than four times like you have been.

Playing chords in root position

Here are all of our chord progressions in root position. You should notice your right- and left-hands moving quite a bit over the keyboard.

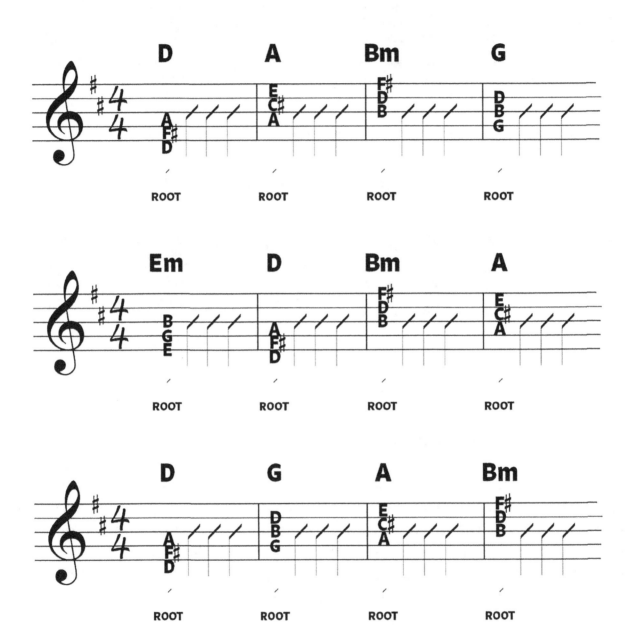

Playing all chords between notes D and C#

Let's use some of our key of D inversions. Place your pencils on the C# and D notes. This should keep each of your progressions between the D and C# notes.

CHORDS BETWEEN D AND C#
-Pencils on C# and D Notes-

91

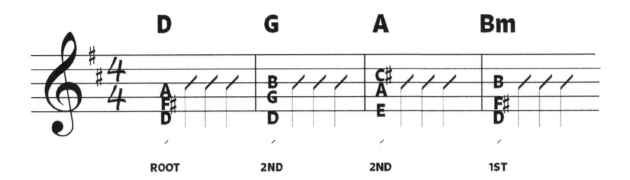

Playing all chords between notes F♯ and E

Move your pencils up two notes to the E and F♯ notes. This set of notes will use your D chord in its first inversion.

CHORDS BETWEEN F♯ AND E
-Pencils on E and F♯ Notes-

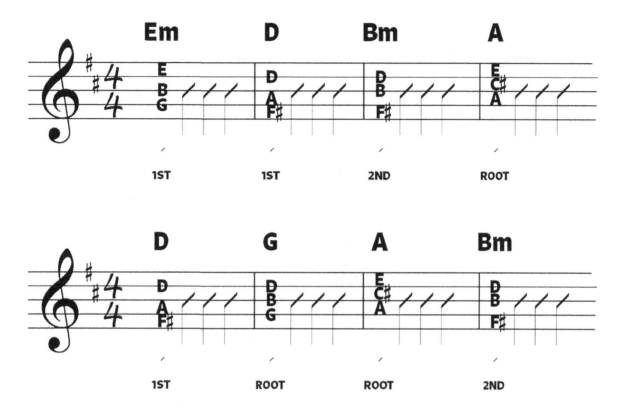

Playing all chords between notes A and G

Last, move your pencils up two more whole steps to the G and A notes. This keeps your progressions between A and G. This last series uses the D chord in its second inversion.

CHORDS BETWEEN A AND G
-Pencils on G and A Notes-

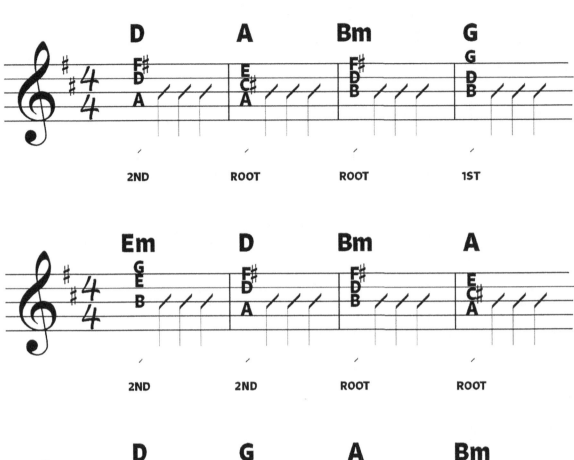

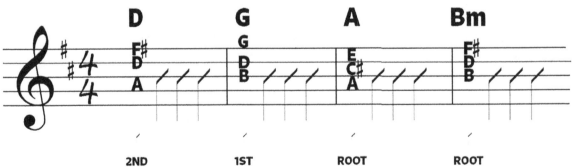

The Key of A

What you need to know about the key of A

One more tick right on the circle of fifths from the key of D is the key of A. We will replace our G natural note with a G#. While this key has three sharp notes, I find it to be one of the easiest, most pleasant-sounding keys. Plus, it's fun to play in.

Notes in the key of A and fingering the scale

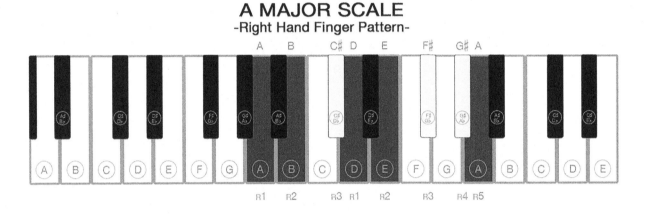

A chord and its inversions

The root chord for this key is A. This is the same A that you used as the 5 chord in the key of D. Here are your finger positions.

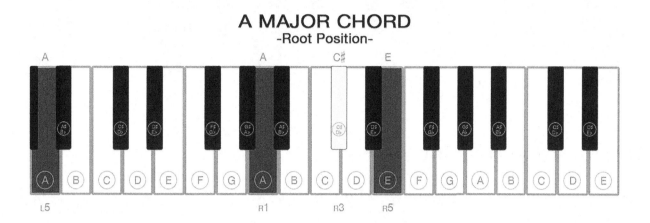

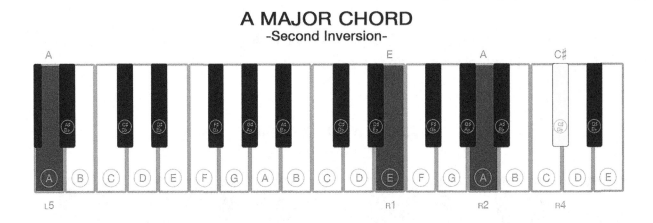

A MAJOR CHORD
-Second Inversion-

Bm chord and its inversions

The 2m chord is Bm. As with the A, this is one of the same chords you played in the previous chapter.

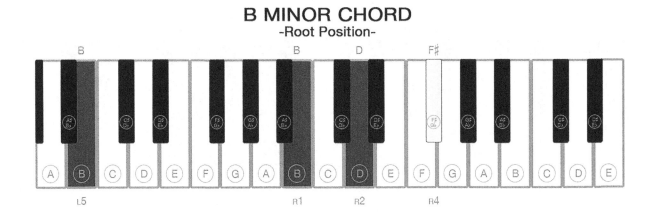

B MINOR CHORD
-Root Position-

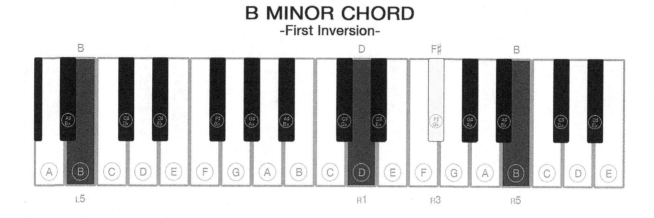

B MINOR CHORD
-First Inversion-

B MINOR CHORD
-Second Inversion-

A/C# chord and its inversions

You've also already learned the A/C# chord. This time it's the 1/3 chord instead of the 5/7 as it was in the key of D. Here are the positions.

A/C# MAJOR CHORD
-Root Position-

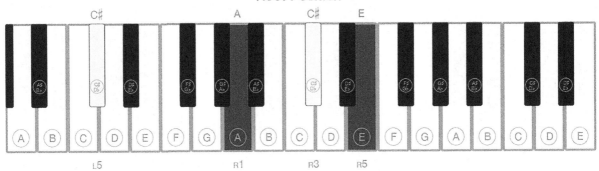

A/C# MAJOR CHORD
-First Inversion-

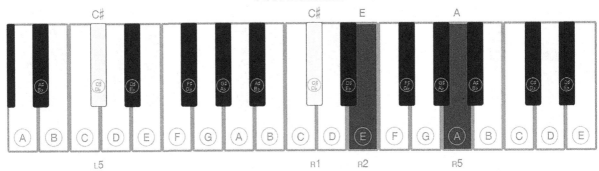

A/C# MAJOR CHORD
-Second Inversion-

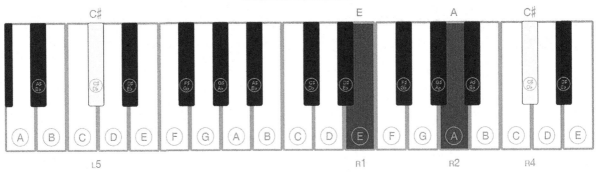

D chord and its inversions

This is the third time you are seeing the D chord. It was the 5 chord in the key of G; the 1 chord in the key of D; and now it's the 4 chord in the key of A.

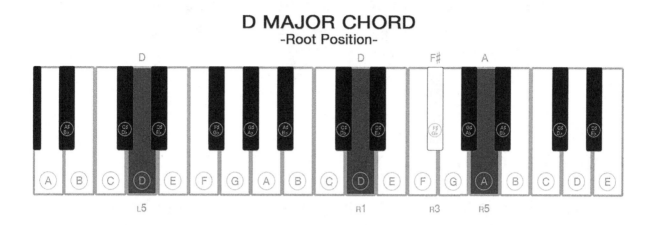

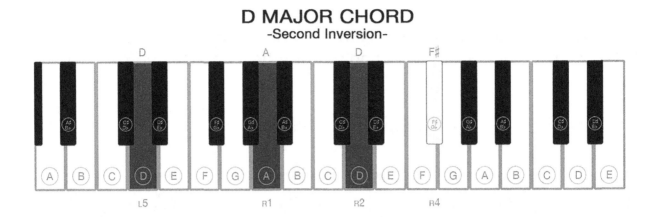

E chord and its inversions

The E major chord is the 5 chord in the key of A. This is the first time we are seeing this one. It will have its own key in the next chapter. You play this similar to the Em chord, but you sharp the third note, G, to a G#. Here is how to play all three positions. You may need to take time learning the stretches for the two inversions.

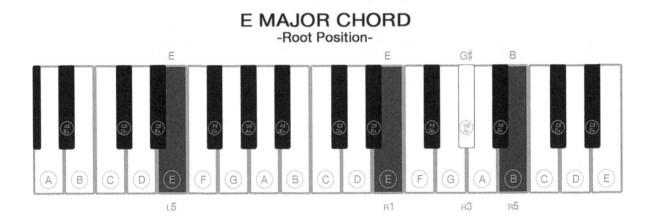

E MAJOR CHORD
-First Inversion-

E MAJOR CHORD
-Second Inversion-

F#m chord and its inversions

The 6m for the key of A is F#m. This is the first chord that we learn that begins with a sharp note. You will need to raise your wrist up to meet the required F# and C# notes. Each position has its own set of stretches and challenges. Do your best to practice each as much as you can during your practice sessions. If you find it frustrating, come back to it the next day. Here is how to play each position.

F♯ MINOR CHORD
-Root Position-

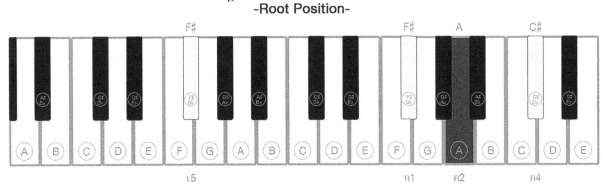

F♯ MINOR CHORD
-First Inversion-

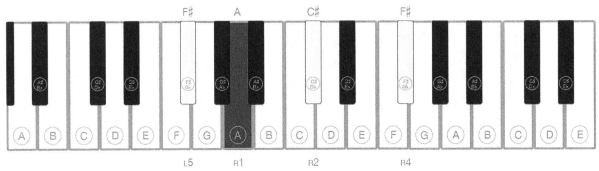

F♯ MINOR CHORD
-Second Inversion-

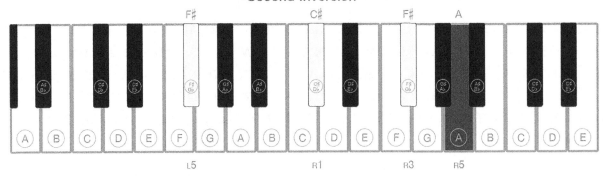

E/G# chord and its inversions

The E/G# chord is the same as an E chord, but the 5 note has been raised to a 7 in the left-hand. The E note is now a G#. Play an E chord, with your pinky finger, L5, and then move to an E/G# by using your middle finger, L3. It will lift the chord without needing to move your left-hand off the keys. Here is how to play all three positions.

Practice progressions

It's time for your practice progressions again. Each key that we move to gets tougher and tougher. I recommend taking your time with each of these progressions as you develop muscle memory.

Playing chords in root position

Play each of our progressions using the root position for each chord.

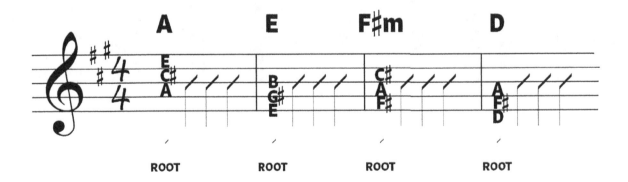

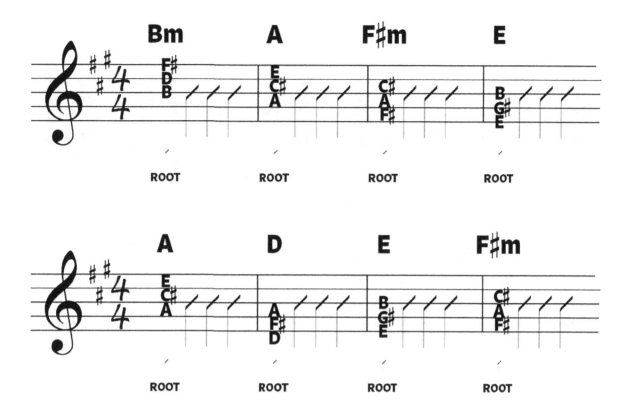

Playing all chords between notes A and G♯

Place your pencils on the G♯ and A notes. This should keep all of your positions between the A and G♯ notes. Notice that all of your 1 chords, A, will be in root position for these progressions. This means that the top note of your 1 chord is the fifth note of the A scale, which is an E note. This is useful when a song's melody hits an E quite a bit.

CHORDS BETWEEN A AND G#
-Pencils on G# and A Notes-

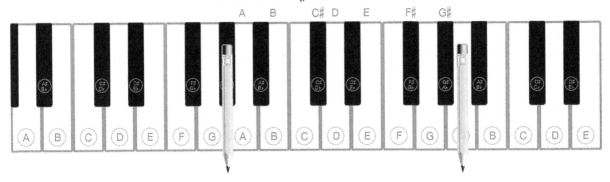

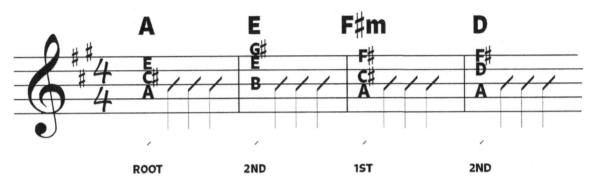

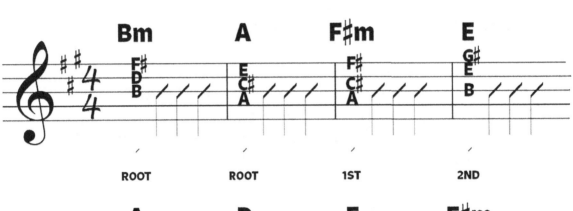

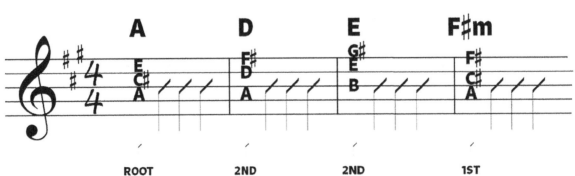

Playing all chords between notes C# and B

Move your pencils up two notes each. They should now rest on the B and C# notes. You may need to angle your pencil to let it rest on the C# key. All of your chords should be played between C# and B. This places the tonic note, A, at the top of the A chord. This is especially helpful when melodies for songs include that note quite a bit.

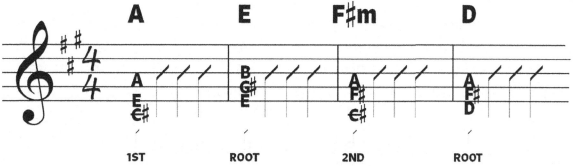

CHORDS BETWEEN C# AND B
-Pencils on B and C# Notes-

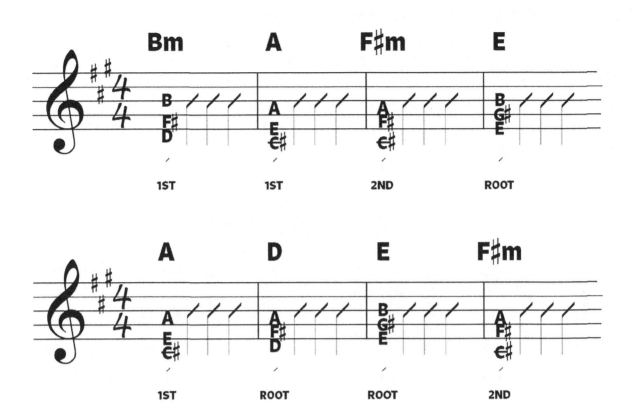

Playing all chords between notes E and D

Our final progressions move the pencils up two more keys. Now they should be placed on the D and E notes. This keeps your fingers between E and D. The third note of the scale, C#, is now on top of the A chord. The third note of the scale is known as the color note, or the note which gives a chord its character.

CHORDS BETWEEN E AND D
-Pencils on D and E Notes-

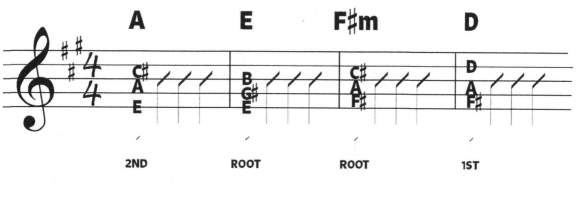

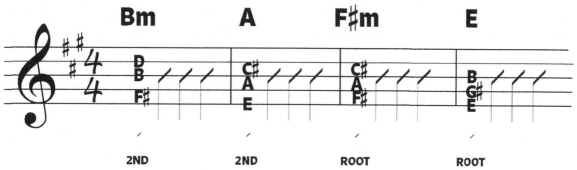

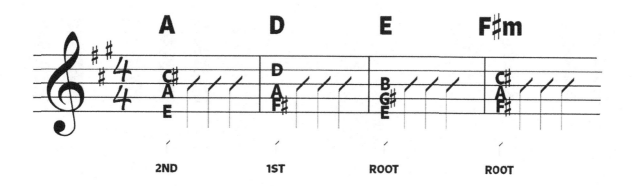

The Key of E

What you need to know about the key of E

The key of E has four sharps in it: F#, G#, C#, and D#. It's four ticks to the right on the circle of fifths. As with the previous chapter, we've added several black keys to our set of naturals. From the key of A, we'll now substitute our natural D note for a D#. Our sharp notes finally outnumber the naturals! Don't let that slow you down. Every key is important. The key of E is known as a guitar key much like the keys of D and G. This is so because guitar players are able to use several of their chords in open position. Therefore, you'll likely find several of your favorite tunes written in the key of E.

Notes in the key of E and fingering the scale

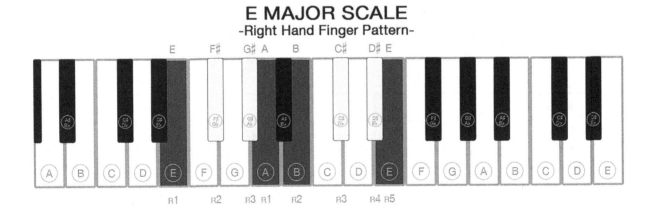

E MAJOR SCALE
-Right Hand Finger Pattern-

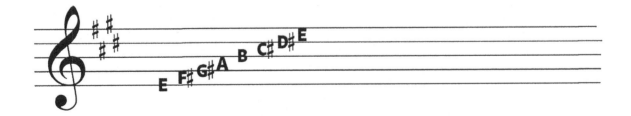

E chord and its inversions

The E, D, and A chords are fingered using the same shapes. By now you should be comfortable with these positions. The E chord, which is the 1 chord in the key of E, is the same chord you learned as the 5 chord in the key of A. Here is each of the positions.

E MAJOR CHORD
-Root Position-

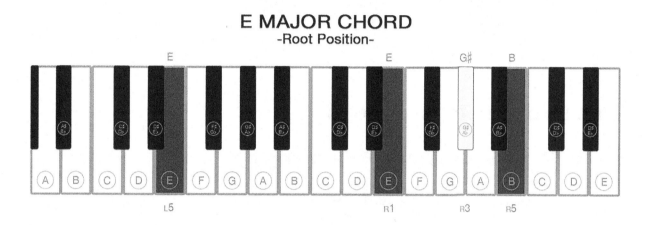

E MAJOR CHORD
-First Inversion-

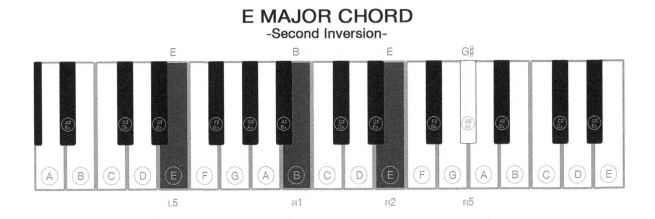

F#m chord and its inversions

The 2m is F#m. This was also the 6m in the key of A.

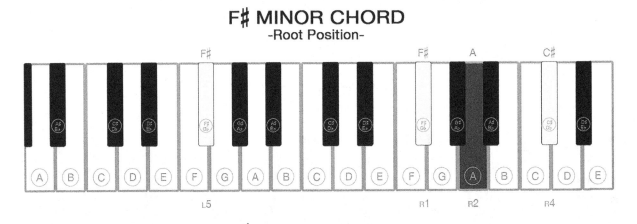

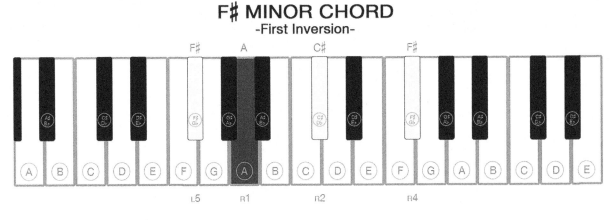

114

F# MINOR CHORD
-Second Inversion-

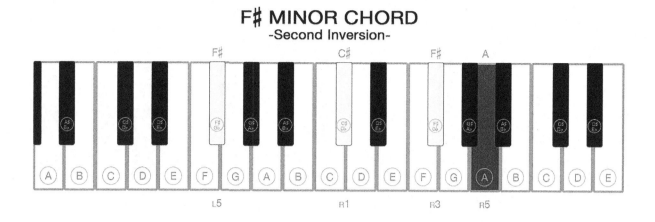

E/G# chord and its inversions

The 1/3 chord is E/G#. This is the same as your 1 chord, E, but the bass note has been shifted up two full steps to a G# note. In my piano diagrams below, I recommend using your left-hand pinky finger, L5, but you are welcome to use your middle finger, L3, instead. This allows you to play an E chord by placing your pinky finger, L5, on the E note and then lift the chord up, by removing your L5 and then striking the G# note with your middle finger, L3.

E/G# MAJOR CHORD
-Root Position-

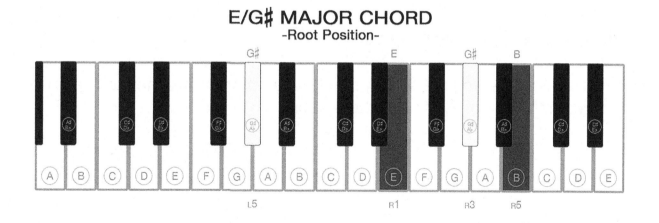

115

E/G♯ MAJOR CHORD
-First Inversion-

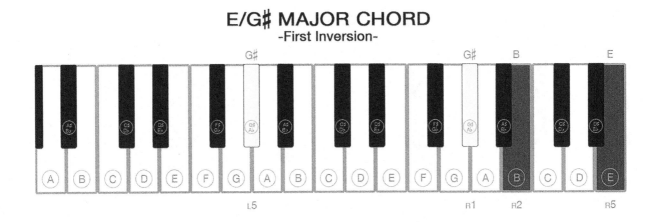

E/G♯ MAJOR CHORD
-Second Inversion-

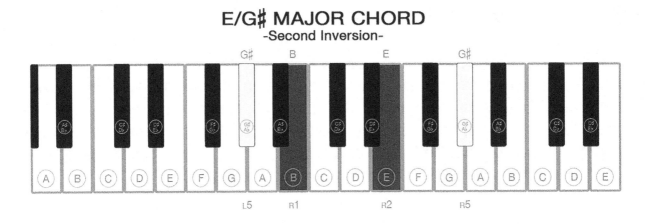

A chord and its inversions

This is the third time you are seeing the A major chord. Here they are again for reference. In the key of E, the A is the 4 chord.

A MAJOR CHORD
-Root Position-

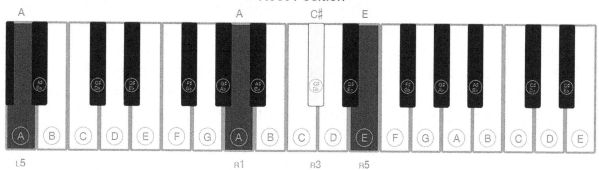

A MAJOR CHORD
-First Inversion-

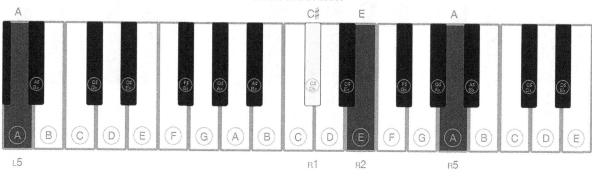

A MAJOR CHORD
-Second Inversion-

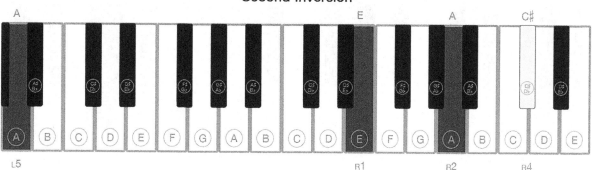

B chord and its inversions

The 5 chord in the key of E is the B major chord. This is the first time we are encountering a B natural chord. In the key of F (Chapter Three), you played a B♭ chord but the two are unrelated. Our B chord has two sharps in it: D♯ and F♯. For most of us, B chords require some finger stretching. Plus they will require time to develop muscle memory. The toughest of these shapes is the second inversion. You must split two black keys with a white key in the middle. Here are the three shapes for the B major chord.

B MAJOR CHORD
-Root Position-

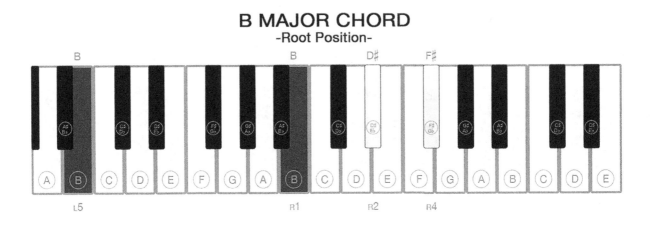

B MAJOR CHORD
-First Inversion-

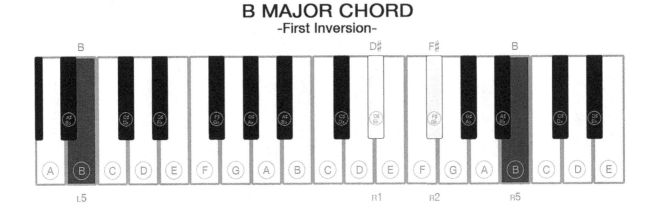

B MAJOR CHORD
-Second Inversion-

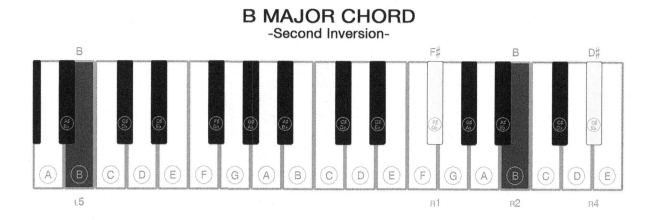

C#m chord and its inversions

The 6m for the key of E is C#m. Like F# and B, you'll need to play two black keys that sandwich a white key while in root position. As before, continue to let your wrist raise upward toward the top of the keyboard to accommodate for the sharp notes. Notice that a C#m and an E chord are nearly identical, save that the B note from the E chord has been raised to a C# for the C#m. Since you've worked through the E chord several times already let it be your guide while learning C#m.

C# MINOR CHORD
-Root Position-

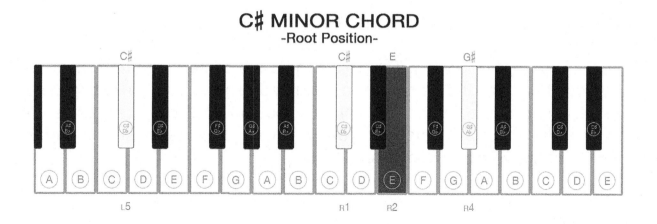

119

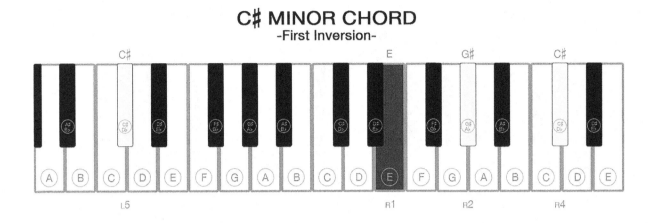

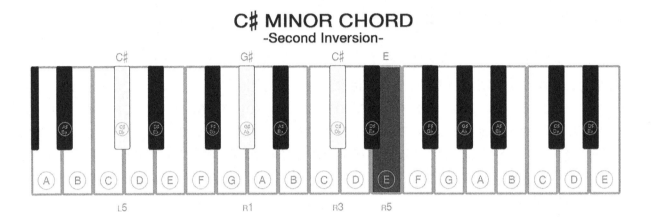

B/D♯ chord and its inversions

The 5/7 chord in this key is B/D♯. This fingers the same in the right-hand as you already have with the B chord. You only need to move your pinky finger, L5, up to a D♯ note instead of the root note, B. You should also try using different fingers to play this bass note with your left-hand. I typically use my middle finger, L3, as we've discussed several times.

B/D♯ MAJOR CHORD
-Root Position-

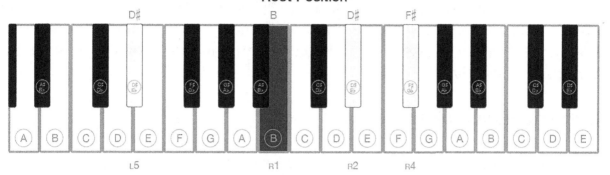

B/D♯ MAJOR CHORD
-First Inversion-

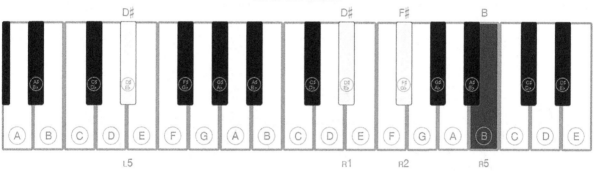

B/D♯ MAJOR CHORD
-Second Inversion-

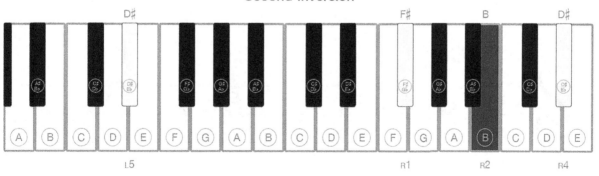

Practice progressions

Let's get down to playing some songs (progressions). Because this key has the most sharp notes so far, give yourself time to get your finger positioning just right. Remember to use the tennis ball technique that keeps your wrist and fingers bent correctly.

Playing chords in root position

Here are each of our three chord fingerings using root position. Because you've played these progressions for five chapters, you could begin to develop your own melody over them. Use the first progression as your verse; the middle progression as a pre-chorus leading you into a chorus; and the final progression as your chorus. If you've never written a song before, this is a great time to start.

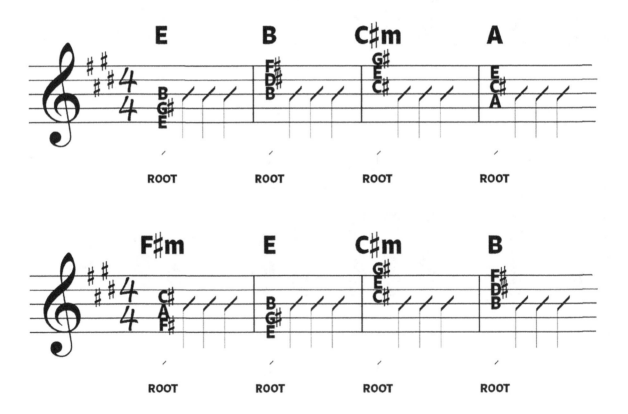

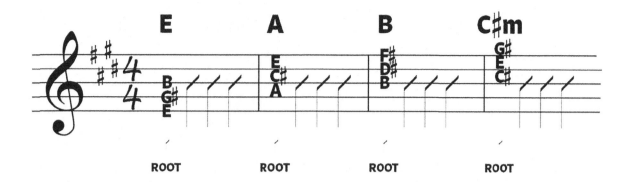

Playing all chords between notes E and D#

Now, place pencils on your D# and E notes. This keeps each of your chords in between E and D#. All of your 1 chords will be in root position, but the others will vary based upon available notes within your pencil boundaries.

CHORDS BETWEEN E AND D#
-Pencils on D# and E Notes-

123

Playing all chords between notes G♯ and F♯

Move your pencils up two steps each. Now, you should be playing between G# and F# notes and your pencils should be on F# and G#. Your 1 chord has been inverted to the first inversion.

CHORDS BETWEEN G# AND F#
-Pencils on F# and G# Notes-

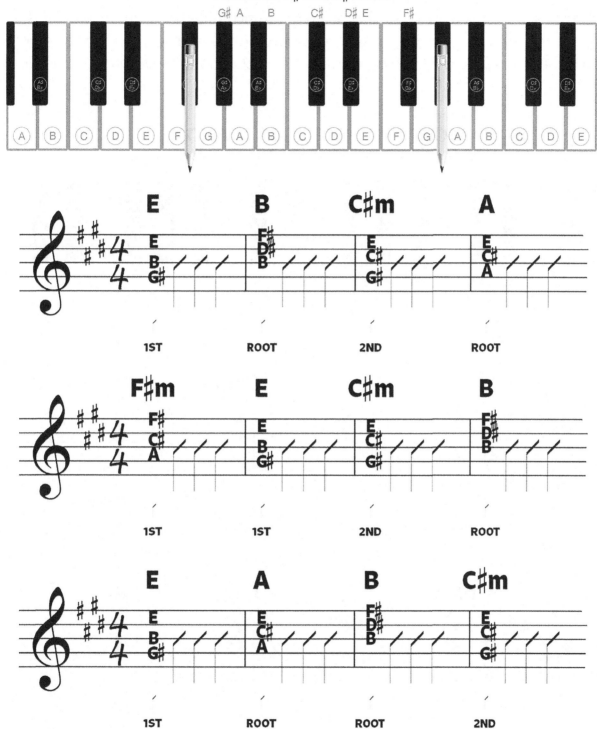

125

Playing all chords between notes B and A

Last, move your pencils up two more whole steps to the A and B notes. All of your chords should now fall somewhere between B and A. Your root position E chord is in the second inversion and all other chords fall within our new range.

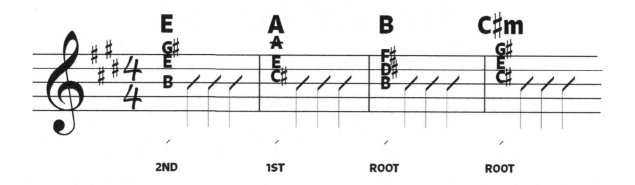

The Key of B

What you need to know about the key of B

Can you believe it? You've made it to the final key in this book! I'm thrilled for you! The key of B is the most difficult we discuss because it has five sharp notes in it. There are only two naturals: B and E. The key of B is difficult for guitarists (because of the many barre chords required) and pianists (because of all the sharps). However, higher male singers (tenors) and lower female singers (altos) tend to like singing in this key because the fifth note of the scale, F#, makes for a powerful chorus melody note. Plus, the high B note, which is the tonic or root note, sounds great as a melody note for female singers. The point here is that you cannot avoid this key. At some point, some of your favorite songs will be played in the key of B and it's worth learning.

Notes in the key of B and fingering the scale

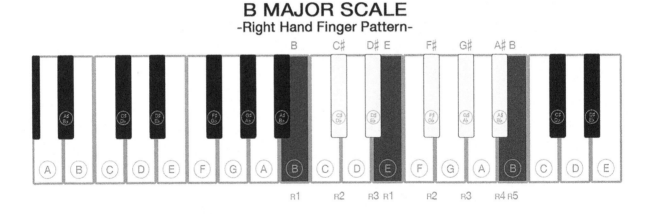

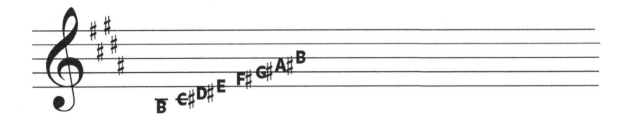

B chord and its inversions

The root, tonic, or 1 chord in the key of B is B major. This was the 5 chord that you learned in the key of E, so you're ahead of the game here. Below are all three positions for reference.

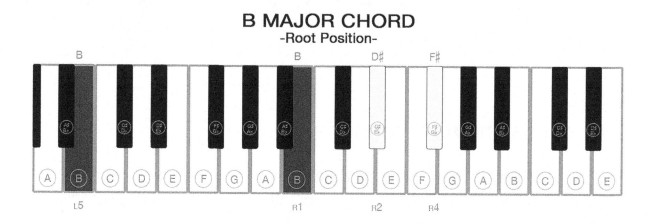

B MAJOR CHORD
-Root Position-

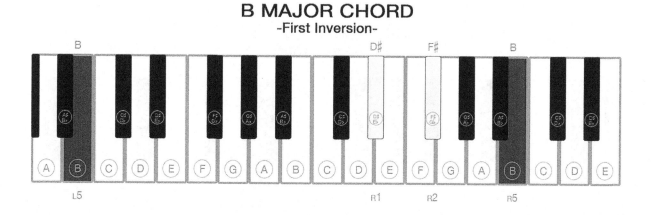

B MAJOR CHORD
-First Inversion-

B MAJOR CHORD
-Second Inversion-

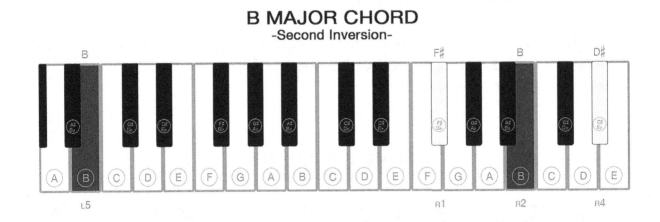

C#m chord and its inversions

Our 2m in this key is C#m. Again, as with B major, you learned this chord in the previous chapter. Instead of it being the 6m chord, it's now the 2m chord in the key of B.

C# MINOR CHORD
-Root Position-

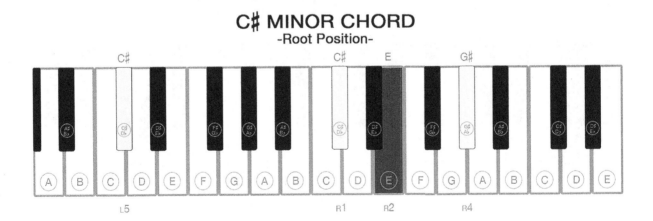

C# MINOR CHORD
-First Inversion-

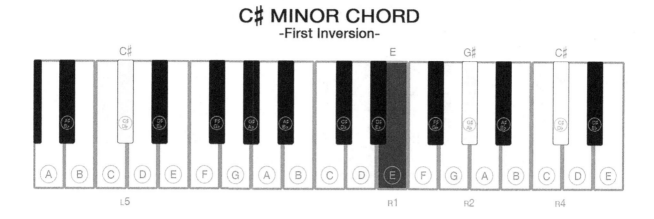

C# MINOR CHORD
-Second Inversion-

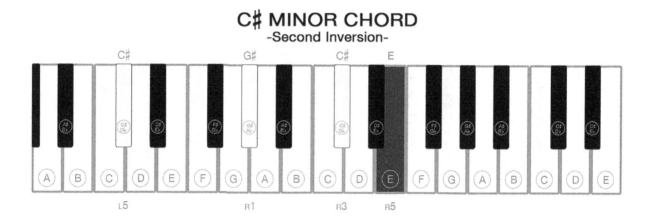

B/D# chord and its inversions

The 1/3 is B/D#. Simply play your B chord and then shift the bass note up from a B to a D#. Here are all three positions. I've diagrammed each of these to move up as you change inversions in the right-hand. You could also begin with your right and left-hands two octaves apart (instead of just one) and move your right-hand down to make the first and second inversions. As you become familiar with the B chord—or any chord for that matter—you should be able to play all of your inversions by moving them up or down the keyboard.

B/D♯ MAJOR CHORD
-Root Position-

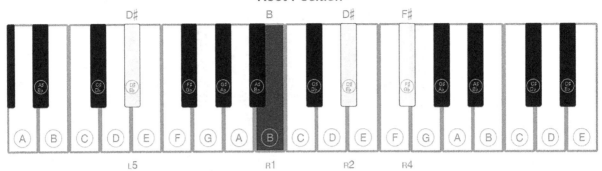

B/D♯ MAJOR CHORD
-First Inversion-

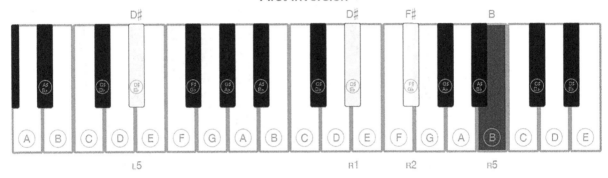

B/D♯ MAJOR CHORD
-Second Inversion-

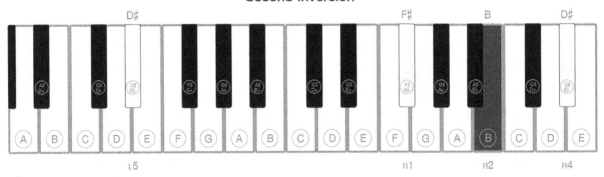

E chord and its inversions

Our 4 chord is an E. This was the 5 chord in the key of A; the 1 chord in the key of E; and now the 4 in B. Each uses the same fingering shapes. In the key of B, the E chord is a pleasant break from needing to play two sharp notes per chord.

E MAJOR CHORD
-Root Position-

E MAJOR CHORD
-First Inversion-

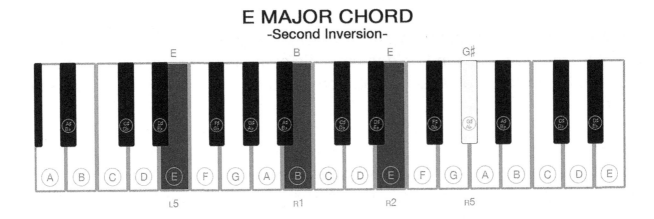

F# chord and its inversions

While you have already learned the F#m chord in the previous two chapters, the key of B calls for an *F# major*. This is the first chord where all of our notes are sharp. While it may sound like it's more difficult, F# major is actually one of the easiest chords in the key of B. Your wrist no longer has to accommodate any white keys. As you build F# major, allow your wrist to move entirely up to meet the black keys that you are playing. When you move to other chords that require natural notes, you'll bring your wrist back down. Here are all three positions for F# major, which is the 5 chord in the key of B.

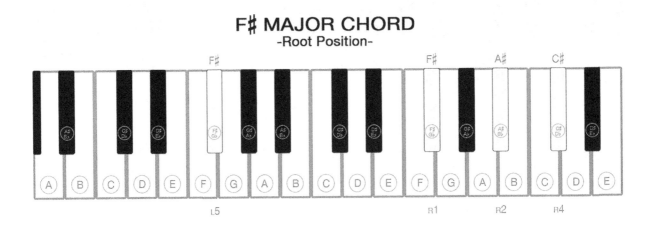

F♯ MAJOR CHORD
-First Inversion-

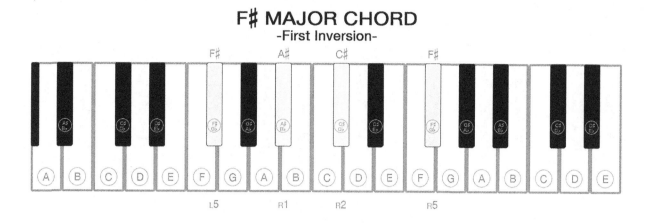

F♯ MAJOR CHORD
-Second Inversion-

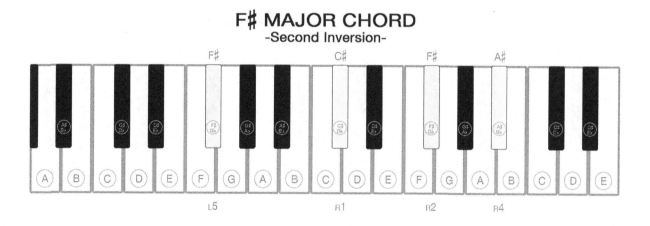

G♯m chord and its inversions

The 6m chord for this key is G♯m. G♯m and B major are nearly identical save that the F♯ note in your B chord has been raised to a G♯ for G♯m. When your muscle memory associates the two it makes learning this chord easier. Here are all three positions.

G# MINOR CHORD
-Root Position-

G# MINOR CHORD
-First Inversion-

G# MINOR CHORD
-Second Inversion-

F♯/A♯ chord and its inversions

Our final chord in this book is F♯/A♯. This is the 5/7 chord for the key of B and we only use black keys. You'll form your F♯ major in the right-hand just as you have two chords earlier when you created the 5 chord, F♯. Here is how to play all three positions for your final chord.

F♯/A♯ MAJOR CHORD
-Root Position-

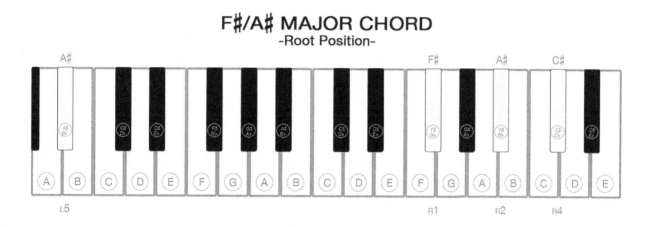

F♯/A♯ MAJOR CHORD
-First Inversion-

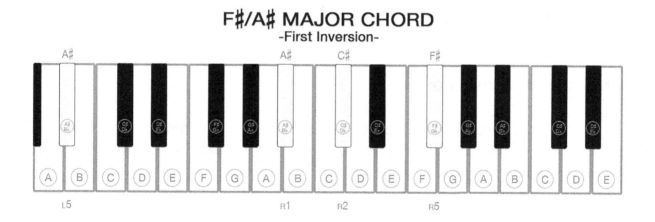

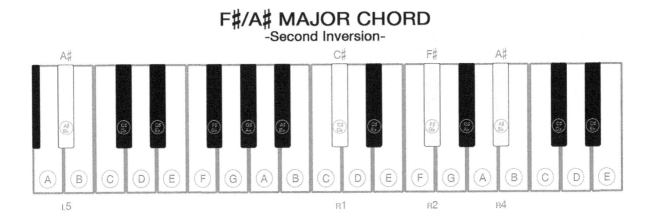

Practice progressions

Let's use all of our inversions by putting them to the test. Since there are so many sharp notes of which to accommodate, take your time learning how your fingers fall correctly onto the keys. This is especially true when you add in the F# and F#/A# chords. You should be coming from a chord with a white key to a chord which has none. This takes practice to get all of your fingers to land in the right place. Move slowly and do your best to develop good habits, keeping great hand and fingering postures as you go.

Playing chords in root position

Here are all three progressions in root position. As I've said all along, you will likely notice the inefficiencies of playing each of these progressions in this manner. However, let's begin with these.

139

Playing all chords between notes B and A#

For the last time, let's pull out our pencils. Place them on the A# and B notes. Remember that you may need to angle the pencil that is placed on your A# note. Using these guides, each progression will land somewhere between the B and A# notes. Each of your 1 chords will be in root position.

CHORDS BETWEEN B AND A#
-Pencils on A# and B Notes-

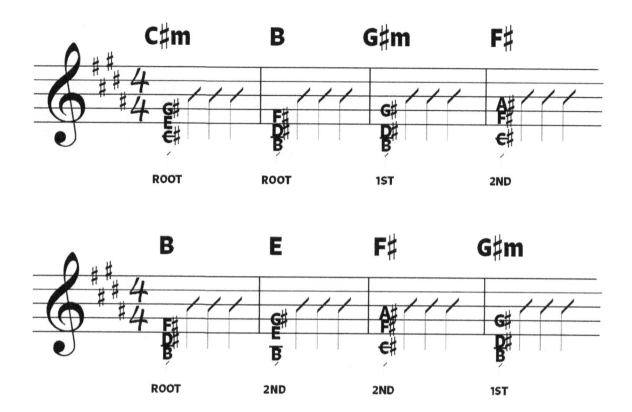

Playing all chords between notes D♯ and C♯

It's time to move your pencils up two whole steps. First, rest the first pencil on the C♯ note while the other goes on the D♯ note. This forces your 1 chord, B, to be in the first inversion.

CHORDS BETWEEN D♯ AND C♯
-Pencils on C♯ and D♯ Notes-

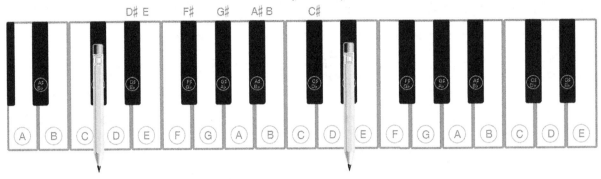

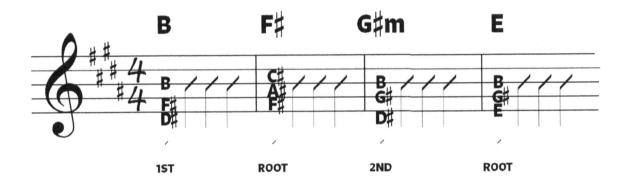

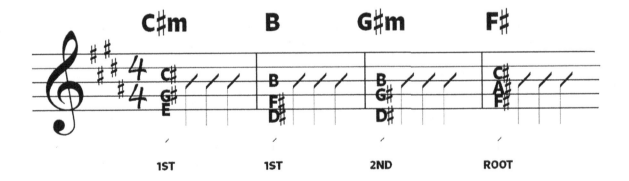

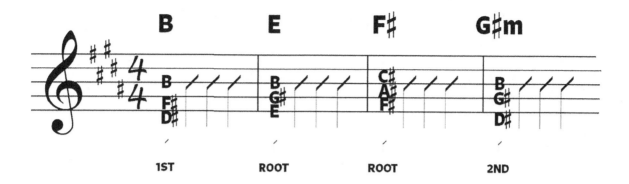

Playing all chords between notes F# and E

Finally, move your pencils up two more steps. They should rest on an E and an F# note. This keeps your chords between F# and E. Your root chord, B, is now in the second inversion.

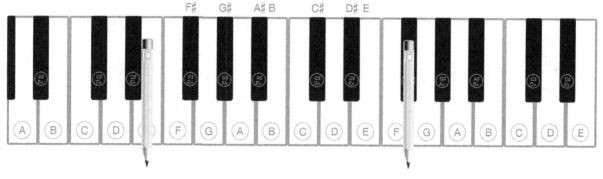

CHORDS BETWEEN F# AND E
-Pencils on E and F# Notes-

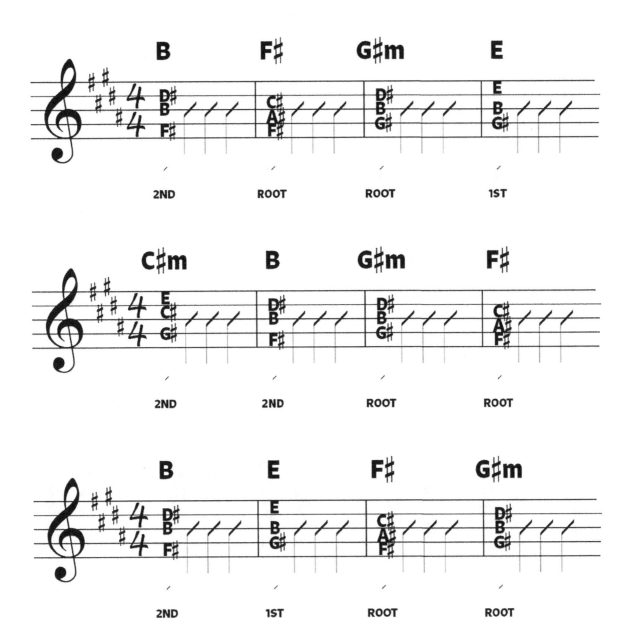

Conclusion

You've just crossed the finish line!

You've done it! You've made it all the way from the key of C to the key of B. Wait, now isn't that alphabetically backwards? I'm exhausted! Aren't you? We have covered quite a bit of material! You should now be able to look over the chords for some of your favorite songs and have no fear. You can now play them! It wouldn't matter if the song was in the key of A or D, you know how to play in any of the natural keys now. This is quite a feat!

So, what about some real songs to play? Here's an answer to your great question. You have played three progressions in seven different keys throughout this book. Did you know that these progressions are the backbones for some of the most famous songs? Even if you don't like the artists below, it's cool to know that you now know how to play their music. For instance, look at this list of famous songs that use our first progression.

Songs using our 1, 5, 6m, 4 progression:

Let It Be (The Beatles)
Auld Lang Syne (Traditional New Year Song)
Let It Go (The Movie *Frozen*)
Innocent (Taylor Swift)
Don't Stop Believin' (Journey)

Fakebooks, the internet, and something called "guitar chords"

I'm betting that you'd love some resources to help you learn some songs. After all, we now have an arsenal of chords with which to use. Here are three that I recommend with which you become familiar. They are fakebooks, the internet, and something called *guitar chords*.

Fakebooks are better known as lead sheets but were coined *fakebooks* several years ago. A lead sheet has chords written on top of a melody line. While you have to do some work to figure out when to play each chord, they are succinct ways of fitting an entire song into two or three pages. You can purchase fake books on Amazon.com or wherever sheet music is typically sold in your area.

Another resource is the internet. The internet is filled with vast amounts of written music that you can play. There is a wide spectrum of quality content too. You could buy professionally transcribed full scores (where every note is written out) all the way to *Back-Woods-Johnny's version of a song he transcribed in his basement*. A quick search using the term "[song title] sheet music" should produce several ways to play the song you're looking for.

You could also search for the term "[song title] guitar chords". While it's true that you're looking to play the song on the piano, using the search term "guitar chords" should yield everything you need to play the song. A guitar chord chart, or just *chord chart*, includes the chords written atop the lyrics. This is also a succinct way to transcribe a song. It's critical to mention that *Johnny in his basement* may be able to publish some chord charts on his webpage, but the chords may not always be correct. These are his best guess as to what the chords should be. As a beginner/intermediate player, you should consider purchasing your sheet music, lead sheets, or chord charts. Then, you'll know that the chords are correct. Plus, you'll know that the writers of the music are being properly compensated.

Appendix

The bonus section

Use the following major scale fingering diagrams to learn how to play octave (eight note) scales for all major keys. This book covers the first seven of these keys, C, G, F, D, A, E, and B. The other keys are just as important and the material of the next book in this series. The keys of C# and F# also have the names D♭ and G♭. They are the same set of notes but have different names for the keys and several notes. Think of it as looking at a key from two different perspectives.

Major Scale Fingerings

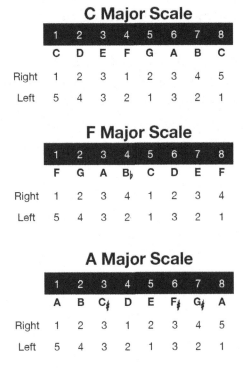

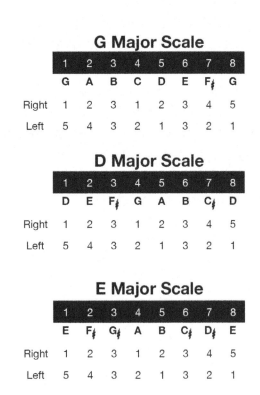

C Major Scale

	1	2	3	4	5	6	7	8
	C	D	E	F	G	A	B	C
Right	1	2	3	1	2	3	4	5
Left	5	4	3	2	1	3	2	1

G Major Scale

	1	2	3	4	5	6	7	8
	G	A	B	C	D	E	F#	G
Right	1	2	3	1	2	3	4	5
Left	5	4	3	2	1	3	2	1

F Major Scale

	1	2	3	4	5	6	7	8
	F	G	A	B♭	C	D	E	F
Right	1	2	3	4	1	2	3	4
Left	5	4	3	2	1	3	2	1

D Major Scale

	1	2	3	4	5	6	7	8
	D	E	F#	G	A	B	C#	D
Right	1	2	3	1	2	3	4	5
Left	5	4	3	2	1	3	2	1

A Major Scale

	1	2	3	4	5	6	7	8
	A	B	C#	D	E	F#	G#	A
Right	1	2	3	1	2	3	4	5
Left	5	4	3	2	1	3	2	1

E Major Scale

	1	2	3	4	5	6	7	8
	E	F#	G#	A	B	C#	D#	E
Right	1	2	3	1	2	3	4	5
Left	5	4	3	2	1	3	2	1

B Major Scale

	1	2	3	4	5	6	7	8
	B	C♯	D♯	E	F♯	G♯	A♯	B
Right	1	2	3	1	2	3	4	5
Left	4	3	2	1	4	3	2	1

B♭ Major Scale

	1	2	3	4	5	6	7	8
	B♭	C	D	E♭	F	G	A	B♭
Right	2	1	2	3	1	2	3	4
Left	3	2	1	4	3	2	1	3

E♭ Major Scale

	1	2	3	4	5	6	7	8
	E♭	F	G	A♭	B♭	C	D	E♭
Right	3	1	2	3	4	1	2	3
Left	3	2	1	4	3	2	1	3

A♭ Major Scale

	1	2	3	4	5	6	7	8
	A♭	B♭	C	D♭	E♭	F	G	A♭
Right	3	4	1	2	3	1	2	3
Left	3	2	1	4	3	2	1	3

C♯/D♭ Major Scale

	1	2	3	4	5	6	7	8
	C♯	D♯	E♯	F♯	G♯	A♯	B♯	C♯
Right	2	3	1	2	3	4	1	2
Left	3	2	1	4	3	2	1	3

C♯/D♭ Major Scale

	1	2	3	4	5	6	7	8
	D♭	E♭	F	G♭	A♭	B♭	C	D♭
Right	2	3	1	2	3	4	1	2
Left	3	2	1	4	3	2	1	3

F♯/G♭ Major Scale

	1	2	3	4	5	6	7	8
	F♯	G♯	A♯	B	C♯	D♯	E♯	F♯
Right	2	3	4	1	2	3	1	2
Left	4	3	2	1	3	2	1	4

F♯/G♭ Major Scale

	1	2	3	4	5	6	7	8
	G♭	A♭	B♭	C♭	D♭	E♭	F	G♭
Right	2	3	4	1	2	3	1	2
Left	4	3	2	1	3	2	1	4

149

About The Author

Why so many people learn music from Micah

The best instructors teach the student, not the curriculum. The curriculum serves as a vehicle for learning. It's a tool of sorts. One of the best parts of teaching music lessons–in this case, piano chording–is the ability to help a student learn at just the right pace. I've found that my job as an educator is to always be encouraging my students to take one step more than he or she may not have taken on their own. The only thing to sort out is at which pace each student performs best.

I've been teaching piano and guitar courses for more than ten years. My emphasis has always been, and will likely always be, in commercial music. While I think classical music is worth studying, I always find myself improvising over the original melodies–even those of the greats, like Beethoven, Brahms, or Bach. It's human nature to explore and I love teaching with the mindset that the music greats of the past are like proven guides. They shouldn't always be copied, but rather those from whom to learn.

Living twenty-five miles from downtown Nashville, TN has provided myself and family privileges in music that I'm certain are not given in every town. You can't throw a stone in Nashville without hitting someone who is personally, or has a family member, in the music industry. Not one of us takes the Grand Ole Opry backstage tour because we all plan to be there as an artist someday. Even if we sing and play music for Jesus as Christian or worship artists, we still likely won't spend the time or money for that tour. We plan to perform on that ageless circle that lands center-stage someday ourselves.

My wife of nearly ten years is glowing brighter every year. We have three kids who keep us very busy and tired. As of the writing of this book, we have another Kennedy (which is my real last name) on the way. We also keep two Yorkshire Terrier dogs who I'm sure my wife would give away for less than the price of two movie tickets. I love them though.

It's an honor to help you work toward your piano chording goals. These new methods may unlock creativity in you that has been buried deep within for years. It's time to let it out.

Blessings,

-Micah Brooks
www.micahbrooks.com
Find me on Facebook, Twitter, LinkedIn, Instagram, and Amazon.com

Connect With Micah Brooks

Signup for Micah Brooks emails to stay up to date

Subscribe to the Micah Brooks Company "Stay Connected" email list for the latest book releases. This email list is always free and intended to deliver high-value content to your inbox. Visit the link below to signup.

www.micahbrooks.com/signup

Contact Micah

Email Micah Brooks at micahbrooks.com/contact. I want to know who you are. It's my privilege to respond to your emails personally. Please feel free to connect.

Please share this book with your friends

If you would like to share your thanks for this book, the best thing you can do is to tell a friend about Piano Chords One or buy them a copy. You can also show your appreciation for this book by leaving a review on Amazon:

www.amazon.com

Follow Micah Brooks:

Facebook: @micahbrooksofficial
Twitter: @micahbrooksco
LinkedIn: Micah Brooks
Instagram: @micahbrooksco
Amazon: amazon.com/author/micahbrooks

If you have trouble connecting to any of these social media accounts, please visit www.micahbrooks.com.

Worship Publishing is a resource website that includes books, daily devotions, music, podcasts, product reviews, and many more recommendations. Use our wealth of staff writers and high-quality guest post content to better your walk with the Lord. This is the website where you can find publishing information for WorshipHeart Publishing, the publisher of this book. Visit: www.worshippublishing.com.

Sing to him a new song;
play skillfully, and shout for joy.

Psalm 33:3 (NIV)

Made in the USA
Middletown, DE
25 July 2022

69986041R00091